Crafting the Digital Experience

**From Idea to App Store:
The Complete Journey of Mobile App Development**

Ryan Matthews

Table of Contents

INTRODUCTION

In today's digital age, the world is at our fingertips due to the remarkable power of mobile applications. Mobile applications have become an indispensable part of our everyday lives, serving us for everything from ordering takeout to hailing a cab, monitoring our fitness levels, to keeping in touch with loved ones. They have sparked inventions, revolutionized industries, and produced innumerable success stories.

Have you ever thought of a fantastic app concept that might completely alter the game? Or maybe you're just getting started in the field of mobile app development and are curious about the nuances involved in transforming a concept into a useful, fully working application? You've come to the right place if you fit into these categories.

Welcome to "Crafting the Digital Experience: From Idea to App Store - The Complete Journey of Mobile App Development." We go on an exciting journey into the world of creating mobile apps with this thorough book, which covers every stage of the procedure. This book is your go-to resource if you're an aspiring business owner with a plan, an experienced developer looking to hone your skills, or just someone who wants to know how the apps you use every day work.

From the first spark of an idea to the exhilarating moment your invention lands in the app stores for the world to see, our journey will take us through the fascinating stages of app development. We'll explore the critical planning, imaginative design, intricate code, careful testing, and smart marketing necessary to ensure your app's success along the way.

This book offers a complete toolkit with case studies, expert advice, and insider knowledge from the industry—it's more than simply a guide. We'll go through the newest developments, industry trends, and ethical considerations to ensure you have the information necessary to deal with the constantly changing field of mobile app development.

This book will enable you to turn your ideas into fully functional mobile apps that connect with consumers and have a long-lasting effect in the digital world, regardless of your experience or background. Are you prepared to start this life-changing adventure? Let's explore "Crafting the Digital Experience: From Idea to App Store - The Complete Journey of Mobile App Development," and unlock the secrets to creating remarkable mobile experiences.

CHAPTER I

Getting Started with Mobile App Development

Understanding the Mobile App Ecosystem

The mobile app ecosystem is a dynamic and ever-evolving landscape that has redefined how we interact with technology and the world around us. Over the course of a few decades, mobile apps have transformed many aspects of our everyday lives, including communication, work, shopping, and entertainment. To grasp the intricacies of mobile app development, one must first understand the ecosystem within which these digital wonders thrive.

The mobile app ecosystem comprises three essential elements: mobile devices, operating systems, and the vast world of mobile applications. These interconnected and interdependent elements create a complex ecosystem that fuels innovation and drives economic growth.

Mobile devices are the hardware that powers the entire ecosystem. These devices have evolved remarkably from the early brick-sized cell phones to today's sleek and powerful smartphones. The proliferation of smartphones has put a sophisticated computer in the pockets of billions worldwide, enabling a multitude of functions beyond mere calls and texts. These devices come in various shapes and sizes, catering to diverse user needs and preferences.

Operating systems (OS) are the bridge between the hardware and the software, serving as the foundation for building mobile apps. Two dominant players, iOS by Apple and Android by Google, have emerged as the leaders in the mobile OS arena. These platforms provide developers with the tools, frameworks, and guidelines to create and optimize apps for their respective ecosystems. The choice of OS significantly impacts app development, as each has its own set of design principles, programming languages, and app distribution channels.

However, the mobile app ecosystem isn't just about hardware and software—it's about the apps themselves, the software applications that bring our devices to life. Mobile apps cover a vast spectrum, from productivity tools and social networking platforms to gaming, education, and healthcare applications. They cater to various user needs and preferences, offering solutions for every aspect of modern life. This diversity has given rise to a vibrant marketplace where innovation thrives, and competition is fierce.

The app stores, such as Apple's App Store and the Google Play Store are central to this ecosystem. These virtual marketplaces serve as mobile app distribution channels, allowing developers to reach a global audience. Through rigorous review procedures, app stores offer customers a way to discover, download, and update apps while also guaranteeing security and quality control.

For developers, app stores offer a unique opportunity to monetize their creations. They can choose from various business models, including free apps with in-app purchases, subscription-based services, and one-time purchases. App stores also provide valuable data and analytics, enabling developers to refine their apps, target specific audiences, and measure their success.

The mobile app ecosystem extends beyond the confines of smartphones and tablets. It encompasses wearables, smart home devices, and other IoT (Internet of Things) gadgets that rely on mobile apps for functionality and user interaction. Apps' smooth integration with these devices improves user experience and raises the bar for what can be accomplished in the digital world.

One of the most remarkable aspects of the mobile app ecosystem is its democratizing effect on innovation. Unlike traditional software development, which often requires significant resources and expertise, mobile app development has become accessible to individuals and small teams. This accessibility has led to a proliferation of indie developers and startups, fostering a culture of innovation and entrepreneurship.

However, the road to success in the mobile app ecosystem is not without its challenges. The competition is fierce, with millions of apps vying for users' attention. Achieving discoverability and standing out in a crowded marketplace is a formidable task. Moreover, technological advancements require developers to stay agile and continually adapt to new trends and capabilities.

Privacy and security are also critical concerns within the mobile app ecosystem. As apps collect and process vast amounts of user data, safeguarding personal information and ensuring secure transactions are paramount. Regulatory bodies, such as GDPR in Europe and CCPA in California, have introduced stringent data protection laws, imposing legal obligations on app developers to protect user privacy.

Understanding the mobile app ecosystem is essential for anyone looking to embark on the app development journey. It's a dynamic world where innovation and creativity collide with the technical intricacies of hardware and software. It's a world where individual developers can create the next viral sensation, and established companies can redefine industries. To succeed in this ecosystem, one must embrace the ever-changing landscape, stay attuned to user needs, and create apps that offer real value and exceptional experiences in our digital age. The mobile app ecosystem is not just a technological marvel; it's a testament to human ingenuity and our ability to shape the future through code and creativity.

Choosing the Right Mobile Platform (iOS, Android, or Cross-Platform)

In the world of mobile app development, one of the earliest and most critical decisions you'll face is choosing the right platform for your app. With the dominance of iOS and Android devices and the emergence of cross- platform development tools, this choice is more complex than ever before. It's a decision that can profoundly impact your app's reach, development cost, and user experience. In this section, we will explore the factors you should consider when deciding between iOS, Android, or cross-platform development, and how this choice shapes the trajectory of your app.

Before delving into the factors that influence platform selection, it's essential to understand the landscape of mobile operating systems. At the forefront are iOS and Android, two giants that collectively dominate the global market. iOS, developed by Apple, powers iPhones and iPads, while Android, developed by Google, runs on a wide array of devices from various manufacturers. These two platforms differ significantly regarding user base, design principles, and development ecosystems.

User base and market share are vital considerations for any app developer. iOS and Android cater to distinct audiences. iOS users are recognized for their intense app engagement and are typically more affluent. On the other hand, Android boasts a larger global market share, making it the go-to choice for reaching a broader audience, particularly in emerging markets. When choosing, you must consider your target demographic and where your potential users are most concentrated.

Each platform has its own design principles and guidelines. iOS prioritizes simplicity, with a clean and intuitive interface. On the other hand, Android offers more flexibility, enabling developers to create highly customized interfaces. Your choice should align with your app's design philosophy. Suppose your app relies on the distinctive iOS look and feel or Material Design for Android. In that case, achieving a consistent user experience with cross-platform development may be more challenging.

The development ecosystem for each platform plays a significant role in your choice. iOS development typically involves using Swift or Objective-C, Xcode as the integrated development environment (or IDE), and adherence to Apple's strict App Store review process. On the Android side, developers use Java or Kotlin, Android Studio as the IDE, and navigate Google Play's less stringent review process. Cross-platform development tools like React Native, Flutter, and Xamarin offer the advantage of writing code once and deploying it on multiple platforms, reducing development time and costs. However, they may have limitations when accessing platform-specific features or achieving optimal performance.

Monetization is a crucial aspect of app development. iOS users have historically been more willing to pay for apps and make in-app purchases, potentially making it a more lucrative platform for premium apps and games. While more reluctant to pay upfront, Android users contribute significantly to ad revenue due to the platform's larger user base. Your monetization strategy should align with the platform's user behavior and expectations.

The platform you select might have a significant impact on the cost and timeline of your development. Because iOS development requires strict adherence to design requirements and requires Apple hardware for testing, it can be more expensive. With its diverse device landscape, Android development may require more extensive testing efforts. Cross-platform development tools can help reduce costs and time, but weighing these savings against potential compromises in performance and platform- specific features is essential.

User acquisition and marketing strategies can also vary based on the platform. iOS users are more likely to discover apps through the App Store, which has stringent guidelines and a curated approach to featuring apps. In contrast, Android users often rely on external sources like web searches and third-party app stores. Your marketing approach should consider these differences and the specific channels that resonate with your target audience.

Maintaining and updating your app is an ongoing process. Users adopt iOS updates more rapidly, making it easier to ensure your app remains compatible with the latest operating system. Android's fragmentation, with various versions in use simultaneously, can pose challenges for compatibility and support. Cross-platform development tools often provide streamlined updates, but you must consider their support for new platform features and timely compatibility with OS updates.

In conclusion, choosing the right mobile platform for your app is a pivotal decision that can significantly impact your app's success. Whether you opt for iOS, Android, or cross-platform development, aligning your choice with your target audience, design philosophy, monetization strategy, development resources, and long-term maintenance plan is crucial. Each platform offers unique advantages and challenges; a thorough assessment of these factors should guide your decision. By making an informed choice, you set the stage for a successful journey in the competitive world of mobile app development, guaranteeing that your app reaches its full potential and delights users on their chosen devices.

Setting Clear Objectives for Your App

The journey of mobile app development is an exciting and dynamic one, marked by creativity, innovation, and the pursuit of creating something valuable for users. However, before diving into the design, development, and deployment process, it's crucial to establish a clear set of objectives for your app. Setting objectives provides a roadmap, guiding your decisions and actions throughout the development process. This section will explore the significance of setting clear objectives for your app and how it shapes every aspect of its creation and eventual success.

At the heart of setting objectives for your app is defining its purpose. Why does your app exist, and what problem does it solve for users? It's essential to articulate a clear and concise purpose that serves as the foundation for all other objectives. Whether your app is designed to streamline a business process, entertain users, or provide essential information, this purpose should be the guiding light that informs every design and development decision.

You need to have a thorough understanding of your target audience's wants and preferences in order to develop objectives that will work. Who are your users, and what are their pain points? What features or functionality will resonate with them? Conducting user research, surveys, and competitor analysis can help you gain valuable insights into user expectations. Your objectives should align with these insights, ensuring that your app addresses real-world problems and offers genuine value to users.

Clear objectives are measurable. They provide specific metrics by which you can gauge your app's success. For example, if your app aims to increase user engagement, a measurable objective might be to achieve a 20% increase in daily active users within the first six months of launch. Measurable goals provide a basis for evaluation and allow you to track progress toward your desired outcomes.

While ambition is admirable, it's crucial to set realistic and achievable objectives. Unrealistic goals can result to disappointment and frustration, both for the development team and stakeholders. Consider budget, resources, and the competitive landscape when establishing objectives. Setting achievable milestones ensures a sense of accomplishment as you progress toward your broader vision.

Once you've defined your app's purpose and objectives, you can prioritize features and functionality effectively. Not all ideas and features will align with your objectives; this clarity helps you make informed decisions about what to include and leave out. Prioritization ensures that your development efforts are focused on elements that directly contribute to achieving your objectives, resulting in a more efficient and impactful development process.

An app's user experience (UX) is crucial to its success. Clear objectives provide a framework for designing an intuitive, user-friendly interface that aligns with your app's purpose. The design should be visually appealing and facilitate users in achieving their goals seamlessly. Every design element, from layout to navigation, should serve the overarching objectives of the app.

Development teams rely on objectives to guide their work effectively. Clear objectives give developers a precise understanding of what needs to be accomplished. This clarity streamlines the development process, reduces ambiguity, and helps teams stay on track. Furthermore, objectives serve as a basis for testing and quality assurance, making sure that the final product aligns with your original vision.

Once your app is live and in the hands of users, objectives become the yardstick by which you measure its success. Regularly analyzing key performance indicators (KPIs) against your objectives allows you to assess whether your app is meeting its goals. If not, objectives also guide the iterative process of improvement. You can identify areas that need enhancement and make informed decisions about updates and new features based on how they align with your objectives.

Clear objectives are a communication tool, aligning stakeholders, including investors, team members, and marketing departments. When everyone shares a common understanding of the app's purpose and objectives, securing funding, allocating resources, and setting expectations is easier. This alignment fosters a sense of purpose and cohesion within the development team and ensures everyone is working toward the same goals.

In the realm of mobile app development, setting clear objectives is not a mere formality but a fundamental process that shapes the entire journey. Objectives provide a sense of direction, enable effective decision-making, and serve as a measuring stick for success. They keep the development process focused, align the team and stakeholders, and ultimately determine whether your app fulfills its intended purpose. Without well-defined objectives, the development process can become disjointed and less effective, leading to missed opportunities and user dissatisfaction.

The art of setting clear objectives lies in striking a balance between ambition and realism. Objectives should inspire and challenge but remain achievable with the available resources. They should be informed by deeply understanding user needs and expectations, ensuring your app genuinely addresses a problem or fulfills a desire. As your app evolves, objectives are crucial, guiding updates, improvements, and adaptations to changing user preferences and market dynamics. In the ever-evolving world of mobile app development, clear objectives are your North Star, guiding you toward a successful and impactful app that resonates with users and achieves its intended purpose.

CHAPTER II

Ideation and Conceptualization

Brainstorming App Ideas

Creating a successful mobile app begins with a single spark of inspiration. This initial idea, often born from a blend of creativity, problem-solving, and market awareness, has the potential to evolve into an app that impacts the lives of millions. However, the ideation process is complex; it involves brainstorming, exploration, validation, and refinement. In this section, we delve into the art of brainstorming app ideas, exploring the techniques, considerations, and creative processes that can lead to the birth of innovative and compelling apps.

The first step in brainstorming app ideas is understanding your motivation. Why do you want to create an app, and what do you hope to achieve with it? Inspiration can come from various sources, such as a personal problem you want to solve, a passion you want to share, or a market gap you want to fill. Understanding your motivation helps focus your brainstorming efforts and ensures that your app idea aligns with your goals and values.

One of the most effective ways to generate app ideas is by identifying pain points and unmet needs. These are problems or challenges people face daily, often serving as the foundation for successful apps. Start by observing your own experiences and those of people around you. What frustrations do you encounter, and how could technology provide a solution? Additionally, conduct market research to identify gaps and opportunities in existing apps or industries.

Your passions and interests can be a fertile ground for app ideas. When you're genuinely enthusiastic about a topic or activity, you're more likely to create an app that resonates with users who share your passion. Whether it's a hobby, a sport, a cause, or a form of entertainment, consider how your interests can be translated into an app that provides value or enjoyment to others.

The world around you is a constant source of inspiration. Pay attention to your daily routines and interactions. Consider how technology can enhance or simplify these experiences. Think about the apps you use frequently and what you appreciate about them. Small improvements or adaptations of existing concepts can sometimes lead to innovative app ideas.

Once you have a general direction for your app idea, it's time to brainstorm and refine it. Various brainstorming techniques can help you explore and expand on your initial concept. One popular method is mind mapping, where you start with a central idea and branch out with related thoughts and concepts. Another technique is "The Five Whys," where you ask "why" repeatedly to dig deeper into the problem or need you're addressing.

Collaborative brainstorming sessions with others can also be highly productive. Different perspectives and expertise can lead to unique insights and innovative solutions. Consider hosting brainstorming sessions with friends, colleagues, or potential users to generate various ideas and perspectives.

While brainstorming is essential for generating app ideas, validating them through market research is equally crucial. Is there a demand for your app concept? Who are your potential users, and what are their preferences and pain points? Research competitors and similar apps to understand the landscape and identify opportunities for differentiation.

Validation might also involve creating prototypes or conducting surveys to gather feedback from potential users. This iterative process helps you refine your app idea and ensure that it aligns with the needs and expectations of your target audience.

Not all ideas generated during brainstorming will be viable or equally promising. It's essential to nurture and refine the most promising ones. Consider the feasibility of development, potential scalability, and long-term sustainability of the idea. Remember that innovation often involves taking risks, which should be calculated and grounded in a solid understanding of the market and user needs.

Iterate on your ideas, seeking feedback and making adjustments as necessary. Sometimes, the most innovative concepts emerge from the evolution of initial ideas through continuous refinement.

Staying informed about current and emerging technology trends can also inspire app ideas. Technologies including augmented reality, virtual reality, artificial intelligence, and the Internet of Things open up new possibilities for innovative apps. By understanding these trends and their potential applications, you can identify opportunities to create cutting-edge solutions.

As you brainstorm app ideas, it's crucial to consider the ethical implications of your concepts. How will your app impact users' privacy, security, and well-being? Will it promote inclusivity and accessibility? Ethical considerations should be woven into the fabric of your idea from the beginning, ensuring that your app benefits users and society as a whole.

Brainstorming app ideas is a creative and exploratory process that sets the stage for developing innovative and impactful applications. It requires curiosity, problem-solving, market awareness, and a genuine desire to create a positive difference in users' lives. Whether your inspiration arises from personal experiences, unmet needs, or emerging technology trends, the art of ideation is a journey that can lead to creating apps that resonate with users and stand the test of time. It's a process that demands creativity and diligence—transforming a mere idea into a powerful tool that enriches, entertains, or empowers users in the digital age.

Validating Your App Idea

In the exhilarating world of mobile app development, the journey begins with an idea—a spark of innovation that has the potential to disrupt markets or enrich the lives of users. However, not all ideas are destined for success, and it's essential to validate your app concept before diving into development. App idea validation is the process of assessing whether your idea has merit, addresses a genuine need, and is worth the time, effort, and resources required to bring it to life. This section explores the significance of validating your app idea and the strategies to ensure your concept is poised for success.

Validation is a crucial step in the app development process because it helps mitigate risks and increase the likelihood of building a successful and sustainable app. Without validation, you run the risk of investing significant time and resources in an idea that may not resonate with users or meet market demands. By validating your app idea, you can save time and money, make informed decisions, and increase your app's chances of achieving your desired goals.

Effective app idea validation begins with thorough market research and competitive analysis. You aim to understand your target audience's needs, preferences, and pain points. Investigate whether similar apps already exist and assess their strengths and weaknesses. Market research helps you identify opportunities for differentiation and ensures that your app addresses a real need in the market.

Engaging with potential users is a valuable validation strategy. Create surveys or conduct interviews to gather feedback on your app idea. Understand how users perceive your concept, what features they find appealing, and whether they would be willing to use or pay for such an app. User feedback provides valuable insights and helps you refine your idea to align with user expectations.

Making a minimum viable product (MVP), also known as a prototype, is a good method to further validate your app idea. Prototypes are interactive mock-ups that allow users to experience the app's core functionality without full development. An app that has been scaled down to its basic features is called an MVP. Both approaches enable you to gather user feedback and test your concept in a real-world context. This iterative process helps you identify flaws, make improvements, and refine your app's concept.

Analyzing your competitors can reveal insights into market demand and user preferences. Examine the top apps in your niche and assess their user ratings, reviews, and feature sets. Look for gaps or opportunities where your app can offer a unique value proposition. While competition can be fierce, it also indicates a demand for solutions in that space.

Before proceeding, evaluate the technical feasibility of your app idea. Consider the complexity of the features you plan to implement and whether the necessary technology or expertise is readily available. Understanding the technical challenges early on can help you assess whether your idea is realistic and achievable.

An essential aspect of validation is assessing your app's potential for monetization. Explore different revenue models, such as in-app purchases, advertising, subscriptions, or one-time purchases, and determine which aligns best with your app's value proposition and target audience. Consider how you will attract paying users or generate revenue, as a viable monetization strategy is integral to the long-term success of your app.

Validation may lead you to pivot or iterate on your app idea. Pivoting involves making significant changes to your concept based on feedback and insights obtained during the validation process. Iterating, on the other hand, involves making incremental improvements to refine your idea further. Be open to both possibilities; adapting to new information can lead to a more successful app.

App idea validation is a fundamental step to creating a successful mobile application. It involves researching the market, gathering user feedback, assessing technical feasibility, and considering monetization strategies. Validation helps you refine your idea, ensure it meets user needs, and make informed decisions about whether to proceed with development. By validating your app idea, you minimize risks, maximize your chances of success, and set the foundation for creating an app that resonates with users and makes a meaningful impact in the competitive app landscape. Remember that validation is an ongoing process that continues throughout the app development journey, guiding your decisions and helping you stay aligned with your target audience's needs and expectations.

Creating a Solid App Concept

Developing a successful mobile app begins long before writing the first line of code. It commences with creating a solid app concept—a blueprint outlining your app's purpose, functionality, and core value proposition. A well-defined app concept is the cornerstone of every successful app, guiding the development process, attracting users, and setting the stage for long-term success. This section explores the significance of creating a solid app concept and the essential elements contributing to its success.

At the heart of every solid app concept lies a clear understanding of users' problems or needs. Your app should aim to address this issue effectively and provide value to users. Start by identifying a pain point or an unmet need in your target market. This problem should serve as the foundation for your app concept, driving every decision you make during development.

You must intimately understand your target audience to create an app that resonates with users. Conduct thorough market research to determine your potential users' demographics, preferences, behaviors, and pain points. Develop user personas representing your ideal users, allowing you to tailor your app concept to their needs and desires. This user-centric approach ensures that your app will genuinely serve its intended audience.

A unique selling proposition (USP) is essential in a crowded app marketplace. Your app concept should clearly define what sets your app apart from the competition. Whether it's a distinctive feature, a more user-friendly interface, or a novel approach to solving a problem, your USPs should be evident in your concept. USPs attract users and provide a basis for marketing and differentiation.

Your app's value proposition is the promise of value it delivers to users. It should be succinctly articulated in your app concept. What benefits will users gain from using your app, and why should they choose it over alternatives? A compelling value proposition attracts users and sets clear expectations for what they can achieve with your app.

A solid app concept includes a detailed outline of your app's core features. These features should directly address the identified problem or need and align with your USPs and value proposition. Prioritize features based on their importance as well as relevance to your target audience. While including a broad range of features is tempting, focusing on a core set allows for a more streamlined and effective user experience.

Sketching the user flow visually represents how users will interact with your app. It outlines the steps users will take to accomplish their goals within your app. This process helps you identify potential bottlenecks or areas where the user experience can be improved. A well-defined user flow ensures that your app's functionality aligns with your app concept and user needs.

While creating a solid app concept is primarily about defining the user experience and value proposition, it's also essential to consider the technical feasibility of your idea. Assess whether the necessary technology and resources are available to implement your concept effectively. This evaluation helps you avoid unrealistic or overly complex features hindering development.

Creating a solid app concept is an iterative process. It often involves brainstorming, feedback, and refinement. Be open to revising your concept based on insights gained from user research, industry trends, or the advice of mentors and peers. Iteration is a valuable part of the concept creation process, as it ensures that your idea remains relevant and effective.

Once your app concept is well-defined, document it thoroughly. Create a concept document encompassing all the abovementioned elements, including the problem statement, user personas, USPs, value proposition, core features, and user flow. This document serves as a reference point throughout the development process, helping to keep your team aligned and focused on the concept's core objectives.

Creating a solid app concept is the essential first step in creating a successful mobile application. It forms the foundation upon which you build your app, guiding every decision and direction. Understanding user needs, defining unique selling points, and crafting a compelling value proposition ensures that your app resonates with your target audience. Moreover, careful consideration of technical feasibility and regular refinement through iteration lead to a concept that is innovative and practical to implement.

A solid app concept is not static; it evolves as you gather insights, conduct user testing, and adapt to changing market conditions. It is a living blueprint serving as your North Star, ensuring your app remains user-centric and aligned with your initial vision. In the competitive world of mobile app development, a well-crafted concept is your most valuable asset, setting the stage for an app that captivates users, fulfills their needs, and stands the test of time.

Market Research and Competition Analysis

In the dynamic and highly competitive mobile app development landscape, success hinges on more than just innovative ideas and technical prowess. Comprehensive market research and competition analysis are paramount to creating an app that resonates with users and thrives in the market. These activities provide valuable insights into user needs, market trends, and the competitive landscape, empowering app developers to make informed decisions and craft winning strategies. In this section, we explore the significance of market research and competition analysis in the context of mobile app development and how these processes can shape your app's success trajectory.

Effective market research begins with a thorough understanding of the market landscape. It involves gathering data and insights about the industry in which your app will operate. Key components of this analysis include market size, growth trends, user demographics, and market segments. By comprehending the broader context in which your app will exist, you can identify opportunities, challenges, and niches that may not be immediately apparent.

One of the primary objectives of market research is to gain user-centric insights. This entails understanding your target audience's behaviors, preferences, pain points, and expectations. Conduct surveys, interviews, and user persona development to create a detailed profile of your ideal users. This knowledge is the foundation for crafting an app that caters to their needs and desires, increasing the likelihood of user adoption and retention.

Market research is instrumental in identifying gaps and opportunities within your chosen market. By examining existing apps and solutions, you can pinpoint areas where user needs are not adequately met or where competitors fall short. These gaps represent opportunities to create an app that offers a unique value proposition and addresses unmet needs.

Competition analysis delves into the strategies, strengths, and weaknesses of existing apps in your niche. Analyze your competitors to understand their user base, monetization models, user experience, and feature sets. Identify market leaders and emerging players, and assess their market share and customer reviews. This analysis helps you identify areas where your app can differentiate itself and provides insights into effective strategies for success.

Studying competitors also allows you to establish benchmarks and best practices. Identify apps that excel in specific areas: user engagement, monetization strategies, or user interface design. By setting standards based on top-performing apps, you can establish clear goals for your own app's performance and user experience.

Market research extends beyond pre-launch activities; it is an ongoing process that continues throughout the app's lifecycle. Gathering user feedback and conducting validation exercises are crucial for post-launch market research. User reviews, ratings, and in-app analytics provide insights into user satisfaction and areas for improvement. You can actively listen to customer feedback and address their demands in order to iterate and refine your app to match changing market preferences.

Monitoring market trends and emerging technologies is another key aspect of market research. Stay informed about the most recent developments in the tech world and how they may impact your app or industry. Technologies like augmented reality (AR), artificial intelligence (AI), or blockchain can open new avenues for innovation and user engagement.

Market research and competition analysis are not static processes; they should inform your app's strategies and roadmaps. Regularly reassess your research findings and adapt your strategies accordingly. For example, if you discover a new emerging competitor, you may need to pivot your approach to remain competitive. Market insights can also guide decisions related to updates, new features, or pivots.

Market research and competition analysis are essential cornerstones of mobile app development. They provide the insights and intelligence needed to make informed decisions, shape strategies, and craft a compelling user experience. By thoroughly understanding the market landscape, gaining user-centric insights, identifying gaps and opportunities, and studying competitors, you set the stage for an app that is innovative and well-aligned with user needs and market trends.

In the ever-evolving world of mobile apps, market research is an ongoing practice that ensures your app remains competitive and responsive to user expectations. It is the compass that guides your development journey, assisting you navigate the complexities of the app market and increasing the likelihood of creating an app that captures the hearts as well as minds of users. Whether you're launching a new app or refining an existing one, robust market research and competition analysis are the keys to unlocking success in the mobile app ecosystem.

CHAPTER III

Planning and Strategy

Defining App Features and Functionality

When embarking on the journey of mobile app development, one of the most critical steps is defining the features and functionality that your app will offer. These elements are the essence of your app, shaping the user experience and determining its value proposition. Whether you're creating a simple utility app or a complex mobile platform, the process of defining features and functionality is both an art and a science. In this section, we explore the significance of this step in app development and the essential considerations that contribute to a successful app.

Every app should have a clear set of objectives that guide its development. These objectives are derived from your initial app concept and define what you intend to achieve with your app. The features and functionality you choose must align closely with these objectives. For example, if your aim is to create a fitness-tracking app, features related to exercise tracking, calorie counting, and progress analysis are essential. Ensuring alignment between features and objectives sets the stage for a purpose-driven app.

User-centric design is at the heart of defining app features and functionality. To create an app that resonates with users, it's crucial to understand their needs, preferences, and pain points. Conduct user research, surveys, and usability testing to gain insights into what your target audience expects from your app. This knowledge should inform the features you select and how they are implemented. A user-centric approach ensures that your app addresses real-world problems and provides value to its users.

Not all features are created equal, and it's necessary to prioritize them based on their importance and relevance to your app's objectives. Begin by identifying core features that are indispensable for your app's functionality and value proposition. These core features constitute the Minimum Viable Product (MVP) and should be developed first. MVP development allows you to launch your app faster, collect user feedback, and iterate based on real-world usage.

Consider the complexity of each feature you plan to implement. Some features may be relatively straightforward, while others may require intricate design, extensive development efforts, or integration with third-party services. Assess the technical feasibility of each feature and weigh it against its potential impact on the user experience. Striking a balance between complexity and user value is essential to avoid overloading your app with unnecessary features.

The design of your app's user interface and the flow of user interactions play a significant role in defining its functionality. A well-designed user experience is intuitive, user-friendly, and aligns with your app's objectives. Pay attention to navigation, information hierarchy, and accessibility to guarantee a seamless and enjoyable user experience. The design should guide users to interact with the app effortlessly and achieve their goals.

Consider your app's future growth and evolution when defining features and functionality. An app should be flexible and scalable to accommodate new features, changes in user needs, and technological advancements. Anticipate potential expansion areas and design your app's architecture to allow for seamless integration of additional functionality in the future. Scalability ensures that your app remains relevant and competitive over time.

The quality and reliability of your app's features and functionality are paramount. Establish extensive quality assurance and testing procedures to find and address any bugs, issues, or usability concerns. Testing should encompass various devices, operating systems, and real-world scenarios to ensure your app performs reliably under different conditions. Quality assurance is an ongoing effort, as updates and changes to your app may introduce new issues.

After launching your app, user feedback becomes a valuable resource for refining and expanding its features and functionality. Monitor user reviews, conduct surveys, and gather feedback to understand the way users interact with your app and their desired improvements. Iteration based on user feedback is a continuous process that allows you to adapt to changing user needs and preferences.

Defining app features and functionality is a pivotal step in the mobile app development process. It carefully balances aligning with app objectives, user-centric design, prioritization, and technical feasibility. A well-defined feature set ensures that your app serves its intended purpose, meets user needs, and provides a compelling user experience. Furthermore, it allows for flexibility and scalability to accommodate future growth and changes in the app landscape.

Successful app development is not just about loading an app with features but about crafting an app that delivers value, solves problems, and delights users. By approaching the process of defining features and functionality with purpose, user-centricity, and adaptability, you set the foundation for an app that not only meets its initial objectives but also evolves and thrives in the competitive world of mobile apps.

Creating a Project Timeline

In mobile app development, turning a concept into a fully functional app is a multifaceted endeavor that demands careful planning and execution. A crucial component of this process is creating a project timeline, which serves as a roadmap for the development journey. A well- structured project timeline helps app developers stay organized, allocate resources efficiently, and meet deadlines. In this section, we delve into the significance of creating a project timeline in the context of mobile app development and explore the key considerations contributing to a successful development timeline.

The foundation of a project timeline is setting clear milestones and objectives. These milestones represent significant checkpoints or achievements that mark progress throughout development. Milestones include completing the app's design, developing core features, conducting beta testing, and preparing for the app's launch. On the other hand, objectives define the specific goals you aim to achieve at each milestone. Establishing well-defined milestones and objectives provides clarity and direction for your development team, ensuring everyone is aligned with the project's goals.

A project timeline involves breaking down the development process into sequential tasks and identifying dependencies between them. Tasks are the individual activities or steps required to reach a milestone. Dependencies denote the order in which tasks must be completed. For example, you may need to finish designing the user interface before you can start developing the app's features. Understanding task dependencies helps you prioritize work and prevent bottlenecks that can delay the project.

Effective project timelines include resource allocation, which involves assigning team members, budget, and other resources to specific tasks. Consider the skills and expertise required for each task and assign team members accordingly. Ensure you have the budget and tools to support the development process. Effective resource allocation ensures that your team can work efficiently and that project costs remain manageable.

Accurate time estimates are critical for creating an achievable and realistic project timeline. Developers, designers, and other team members should provide time estimates for their respective tasks based on their expertise and experience. It's essential to account for unforeseen challenges or delays that may arise during the development process. While optimism is valuable, be cautious of over-optimistic timeframes, which can lead to unrealistic expectations and project setbacks.

No project timeline is immune to unexpected obstacles or changes in priorities. Contingency planning involves preparing for these contingencies and having a plan in place to address them. Identify potential risks impacting the timeline, such as technical issues, resource shortages, or scope changes. Develop strategies to mitigate these risks and plan how to proceed if they occur. Contingency planning allows you to adapt to unforeseen challenges while minimizing disruption to the project.

A project timeline is not a static document but a dynamic tool that requires regular monitoring and communication. Establish a system for tracking progress and updating the timeline as tasks are completed or delayed. Call frequent team meetings to review the status, resolve problems, and revise the timeframe as needed. Effective communication keeps everyone involved in the project informed and on the same page regarding the timeline's goals.

User testing and iteration are integral to the project timeline, especially in mobile app development. Allocate time for beta testing and gather user feedback to identify areas for ´improvement. Iteration involves making refinements and adjustments based on user feedback to enhance the app's usability and functionality. This iterative process should be integrated into the timeline to ensure the app meets user expectations and quality standards.

Creating a project timeline is an essential aspect of successful mobile app development. It provides a structured framework for planning, executing, and monitoring development. A well-designed timeline sets clear milestones and objectives, sequences tasks, allocates resources, and includes realistic time estimates. Additionally, it accounts for contingency planning and integrates user testing and iteration to ensure that the final app meets user needs and quality standards.

A well-planned project timeline aids in resource allocation, keeps developers organized and on schedule, and ensures that a high-quality app is delivered on time. It is a dynamic tool that evolves with the project, adapting to changes and challenges as they arise. In the ever-evolving world of mobile app development, a well-structured project timeline is your compass, guiding you toward a successful app launch and a satisfied user base.

Budgeting for Your App

The development of a mobile app is a dynamic journey that involves a range of activities, from conceptualization and design to coding and launch. One critical aspect that underpins the success of this journey is budgeting. Properly budgeting for your app is essential to ensure that your project remains financially sustainable, stays on track, and meets your objectives. This section explores the significance of budgeting for mobile app development and discusses the key considerations that will help you create a realistic and effective budget.

Before diving into budgeting, it's crucial to understand your app's scope clearly. What features and functionality will it include? Will it be available on multiple platforms (iOS, Android, etc.)? Is it a simple utility app or a complex, data-intensive platform? The scope of your app directly impacts the budget, as more extensive and complex projects require greater resources.

Development costs encompass various expenses, including personnel, software, hardware, and third-party services. You must allocate funds for developers, designers, and quality assurance testers. Licensing fees for development tools and software may also be necessary. Additionally, consider the cost of hardware, such as devices for testing, and any cloud hosting or backend services required for your app.

Aesthetics and user experience (UX) are crucial aspects of mobile app development. Allocating a portion of your budget to app design ensures that your app is visually appealing and user-friendly. Hire experienced designers who can create an intuitive and engaging user interface. Your app's design quality can significantly impact user satisfaction and adoption.

Even the most exceptional apps need effective marketing and promotion to reach their target audience. Allocate funds for marketing activities, including app store optimization (ASO), advertising campaigns, social media marketing, and public relations efforts. A well-executed marketing strategy can significantly boost your app's visibility and user acquisition.

Quality assurance is a critical phase of app development and comes with its own budgetary requirements. You'll need to allocate funds for testing devices, software tools, and the salaries of quality assurance professionals.

Thorough testing ensures that your app is bug-free, reliable, and meets user expectations.

Your app's journey doesn't end with its launch; maintenance and updates are ongoing processes that require budgetary provisions. These costs include bug fixes, security updates, compatibility updates for new devices and operating systems, and the development of new features or enhancements based on user feedback.

Unforeseen challenges and changes in project scope can arise during app development. To mitigate these risks, it's wise to allocate a contingency budget. Contingency funds provide a safety net for handling unexpected expenses, ensuring your project can adapt and overcome unforeseen obstacles without derailing the entire budget.

Consider your app's revenue model when budgeting. Will your app be free with in-app purchases, subscription-based, or ad-supported? The chosen monetization strategy may impact your budget allocation, as you may need to invest in additional features or advertising to support your revenue model.

Budgeting for your app isn't just about spending money; it's also about analyzing the potential return on investment (ROI). Calculate the expected revenue and profits your app will likely generate once launched. Compare these projections to your budgeted expenses to ensure your app's development remains financially viable.

Budgeting for your app is a critical step in guaranteeing the success of your mobile app development project. It involves understanding the scope of your app, identifying development costs, allocating resources for design and user experience, planning for marketing and promotion, and providing for ongoing maintenance and updates. A contingency budget safeguards against unforeseen challenges, while a well-considered revenue model and

ROI analysis help ensure your project's financial sustainability.

Effective budgeting is not just about setting aside funds; it's about making strategic financial decisions that align with your app's objectives and potential for success. Creating a realistic and comprehensive budget sets the stage for a mobile app development journey that is financially sound, on track, and well-positioned for achieving your goals and delighting users.

Selecting the Right Development Team

Behind every successful mobile app, there is a dedicated and skilled development team that turns ideas into reality. Selecting the right development team is one of the most critical decisions you'll make during the app development journey. The team you choose will bring your vision to life and play a significant role in determining the app's quality, efficiency, and success. This section explores the importance of selecting the right development team for your mobile app project and provides insights into the key considerations for making this crucial choice.

The development team is the driving force behind the creation of your mobile app. They are responsible for writing code, designing the user interface, ensuring functionality, and conducting quality assurance to deliver a polished and functional product. The team's expertise, experience, and collaboration are pivotal in shaping the app's performance and user experience.

Before you start searching for a development team, clearly defining your project's requirements is essential. What platforms (iOS, Android, cross-platform) will your app support? What are the core features and functionality you expect from your app? Do you need specialized augmented reality (AR), machine learning, or blockchain integration skills? Having a well-defined project scope and requirements will help you identify the specific expertise your development team needs.

When selecting a development team, expertise and experience are paramount. Look for a team with an established history of success in developing mobile apps that align with your project's goals. Investigate their portfolio and past projects to assess their work's quality and ability to deliver on time and within budget. Consider their experience with similar apps or industries, as this can provide valuable insights into their suitability for your project.

Mobile app development encompasses many skills, from frontend and backend development to design, user experience (UX), and quality assurance. Depending on your app's complexity and requirements, you may need specialists in specific areas. Ensure that your development team possesses the requisite skillset and specializations to meet your project's unique demands. If your app involves advanced technologies or features, such as machine learning algorithms or real-time multiplayer functionality, ensure the team has the expertise to implement them effectively.

Effective teamwork and collaboration are essential for the success of your app development project. A cohesive and communicative team can streamline the development process, address challenges promptly, and ensure everyone is aligned with project goals. During the selection process, assess the team's communication skills, responsiveness, and ability to work together effectively. Consider their willingness to involve you in the development process, provide updates, and incorporate your feedback.

References and reviews from past clients are valuable indicators of a development team's reputation and reliability. Contact with their former clients to find out about their impressions of the team and how satisfied they were with the work they did. Insights regarding the team's performance and client relationships can also be gained from online reviews and testimonials. A positive track record and client feedback are strong indicators of a trustworthy and capable team.

Understanding the development team's process and methodology is crucial for project planning and execution. Inquire about their development approach, project management methods, and tools they use for collaboration and communication. A well-defined and organized development process like Agile or Scrum can contribute to efficient project management and successful outcomes.

While cost is a factor, it should not be the sole determinant when selecting a development team. Quality and expertise often come with a price, and investing in a skilled team can yield better long-term results. However, ensuring that the team's pricing aligns with your budget constraints and project scope is essential. Be transparent about your budget, and discuss pricing structures, payment schedules, and any potential additional costs upfront.

Selecting the right development team is pivotal in the mobile app development journey. The team's expertise, experience, skillset, collaboration dynamics, and reputation all contribute to the success of your project. By defining your project's requirements, conducting thorough research, and considering factors such as team dynamics and development methodologies, you can make an informed choice that aligns with your project's goals and objectives.

Remember that your development team is not just a service provider but your partners in bringing your app vision to life. A well-chosen team can enhance the quality of your app, streamline the development process, and increase your app's chances of achieving success in the competitive mobile app landscape.

CHAPTER IV

Designing Your Mobile App

User-Centered Design Principles

User-centered design (UCD) is a fundamental approach that places users' needs, preferences, and behaviors at the forefront of the design process. In the world of mobile app development, UCD principles play a pivotal role in creating apps that are not only visually appealing but also intuitive, user-friendly, and effective in meeting user needs. In this section, we delve into the significance of user-centered design principles and explore the key principles that guide the creation of exceptional mobile app experiences.

User-centered design is more than just a design philosophy; it's a holistic approach encompassing the entire app development process. At its core, UCD seeks to ensure that an app's design and functionality align with its intended users' expectations and behaviors. This approach places users at the center of decision-making, driving the creation of products that are more likely to be embraced and appreciated by their target audience.

Principle 1: User Research

User research is the foundation of UCD. It involves gathering insights about your target audience's behaviors, preferences, and needs. Through methods like surveys, interviews, and usability testing, designers acquire a deep understanding of their users. This knowledge informs design choices, ensuring the app addresses real user pain points and meets their expectations.

Principle 2: Design for Usability

Usability is a core tenet of UCD. Apps should be designed to be easy to learn, efficient to use, and free from unnecessary complexity. This involves creating intuitive user interfaces, clear navigation paths, and straightforward interactions. A focus on usability ensures that users can achieve their goals within the app without frustration or confusion.

Principle 3: Feedback and Iteration

User-centered design is an iterative process that welcomes feedback and refinement. Designers should seek user input throughout the development cycle, from initial prototypes to the final product. User feedback helps identify usability issues and areas for improvement, enabling designers to make informed adjustments and enhancements.

Principle 4: Accessibility and Inclusivity

Designing with accessibility in mind is a fundamental UCD principle. Apps should be usable by individuals with diverse abilities, including those with disabilities. This involves considering screen reader compatibility, keyboard navigation, and text legibility. Inclusivity ensures that a broader user base can enjoy your app.

Principle 5: Consistency and Familiarity

Consistency in design elements and interactions contributes to a seamless user experience. Users should encounter familiar patterns and conventions, such as standardized navigation menus or common iconography. Consistency reduces cognitive load and helps users feel comfortable and confident while using the app.

Principle 6: Minimalism and Clarity

The principle of minimalism advocates for simplicity and clarity in design. Avoid clutter and unnecessary elements that can distract users from their goals. Prioritize essential information and actions, presenting them clearly and concisely. Minimalistic design enhances the user's ability to focus on what matters most.

Principle 7: Flexibility and Personalization

Not all users are the same, and UCD recognizes the importance of flexibility and personalization. Apps should offer options and settings that allow users to customize their experience to their preferences. Personalization can include theme customization, content filters, or notification settings.

Principle 8: Performance and Speed

App performance is integral to user satisfaction. Users expect apps to be responsive and swift in their interactions. Slow loading times or laggy responses can lead to frustration and abandonment. UCD principles emphasize optimizing app performance for a smooth and efficient user experience.

Principle 9: User-Centric Content

Content should be structured and presented in a user-centric way. Consider the user's goals and motivations when organizing and presenting information. Tailor content to address their needs and interests, ensuring that it is easily accessible and relevant.

User-centered design principles are at the heart of creating mobile apps that resonate with users and stand out in the competitive app landscape. These principles emphasize understanding users through research, designing for usability, welcoming feedback, and promoting inclusivity and accessibility. By adhering to UCD principles, app developers can make products that meet user needs and provide delightful, efficient, and meaningful experiences. User-centered design isn't just a design philosophy; it's a philosophy of creating apps that truly serve and connect with their users.

Wireframing and Prototyping

Wireframing and prototyping are foundational steps in the journey of mobile app development. They serve as the building blocks, laying out the visual and functional framework upon which the final app will be constructed. In this section, we explore the significance of wireframing and prototyping in the app development process and how these essential tools shape the blueprint of mobile apps.

Wireframing is akin to the architectural blueprint of a building. It focuses on the structure and layout of the user interface (UI) without delving into design aesthetics. Wireframes are typically created using basic shapes, lines, and placeholders to represent the app's elements, such as buttons, menus, and content sections. They outline the spatial arrangement of these elements, guiding designers and developers in crafting a logical and user-friendly interface.

Wireframing offers several critical advantages. Firstly, it offers a clear visual representation of the app's layout and flow, allowing stakeholders to visualize the user's journey through the app. This visualization aids in identifying potential usability issues or design flaws early in the process, saving time and resources. Secondly, wireframes are a reference point for collaboration among team members, including designers, developers, and project managers. They ensure that everyone is aligned on the app's structure and functionality. Lastly, wireframes offer a cost-effective means of testing and refining ideas before investing heavily in development. By soliciting feedback on wireframes, developers can make informed design decisions and prioritize user needs.

While wireframes focus on static layouts, prototypes breathe life into an app's interactivity. Prototyping allows designers and developers to create functional representations of the app, complete with user interactions and transitions. Users can interact with the prototype as if it were the real app, providing invaluable insights into the user experience (UX). Prototypes often include clickable buttons, navigation paths, and interactive elements that mimic the actual app's behavior.

Prototyping goes beyond static wireframes, offering several unique benefits. Firstly, it allows stakeholders to experience the app's functionality firsthand, making evaluating its usability and effectiveness easier. Users can provide feedback on the app's flow, navigation, and interaction design, helping to refine the user experience. Secondly, prototypes serve as a powerful tool for user testing and validation. Early testing with real users can uncover issues or pain points that may not be apparent in wireframes alone. This iterative feedback loop ensures that the app aligns more closely with user needs and expectations. Lastly, prototypes facilitate effective communication between design and development teams. Developers can better understand the app's interactive requirements, streamlining the development process and reducing misunderstandings.

In the app development process, wireframing and prototyping work in tandem. Wireframes create the initial structural foundation, defining the app's placement and hierarchy of elements. Once the wireframes are established, prototyping adds the interactive layer, allowing designers and developers to bring user interactions to life. This synergy between wireframes and prototypes enables a comprehensive and user-centric design approach.

Wireframing and prototyping are vital steps in the mobile app development journey. Wireframes create the structural blueprint of the app's user interface, emphasizing layout and functionality. Conversely, prototypes breathe life into the app, allowing for interactive user experiences and usability testing. Together, these tools form a dynamic duo that guides app designers and developers in creating user-friendly, effective, and visually appealing mobile applications. By embracing wireframing and prototyping, app development teams can save time, reduce costs, and, most importantly, create apps that resonate with users and deliver exceptional user experiences.

UI/UX Design Best Practices

In the world of mobile app development, the success of an application often hinges on the quality of its user interface (UI) and user experience (UX) design. UI/UX design best practices serve as guiding principles that help designers create apps that are not only visually appealing but are also intuitive, user-friendly, and capable of delivering seamless experiences. In this section, we delve into the significance of UI/UX design best practices and explore key principles that empower designers to craft exceptional user experiences.

UI design pertains to an app's visual elements and layout—how it looks and how users interact with it. On the other hand, UX design is concerned with the overall user experience—the ease of use, efficiency, and satisfaction derived from using the app. Effective UI/UX design balances aesthetics and functionality, ensuring that an app is visually engaging and user-centric.

Simplicity is a cornerstone of effective UI/UX design. A cluttered and complex interface can overwhelm users, leading to confusion and frustration. Minimalist design principles advocate for removing extraneous elements, and focusing on what's essential. Strive for clean, uncluttered layouts, intuitive navigation, and a concise presentation of information. Simplicity enhances usability and guides users seamlessly through the app.

Maintaining consistency across different devices and operating systems is crucial in today's multi-platform landscape. Users expect a harmonious experience whether they're using an iOS, Android, or web app. Designers should adhere to platform-specific design guidelines and create responsive designs that adjust to various screen sizes and orientations. Consistency in branding, typography, and user interactions reinforces a cohesive and recognizable user experience.

Content and navigation should prioritize the user's needs and goals. Arrange content logically, keeping the most critical information readily accessible. Implement intuitive navigation that guides users effortlessly through the app. Consider the user's mental model—how they expect to interact with the app—and align the design with those expectations. User-centric content and navigation enhance usability and reduce cognitive load.

Visual hierarchy establishes the relative importance of elements within the app. Using typography, color, and contrast effectively directs users' attention to key content and actions. Important information should stand out, while secondary elements recede into the background. Proper typography ensures readability and legibility, enhancing the overall user experience.

Feedback mechanisms keep users informed about their actions and the app's response. Provide visual, auditory, or tactile feedback when users interact with UI elements. Instantaneous response times create a sense of fluidity and responsiveness, contributing to a positive UX. Additionally, clearly communicate errors and success messages to guide users' interactions.

User testing is an essential part of the UI/UX design process. It entails gathering feedback from real users to evaluate the app's usability and identify pain points. Based on user feedback, Iterative design allows designers to refine the app continuously. User testing uncovers issues that may not be apparent during the design phase and ensures that the final product aligns closely with user expectations.

Designing with accessibility in mind ensures that the app is usable by individuals with diverse abilities. Consider screen reader compatibility, keyboard navigation, and text legibility. Inclusivity in design ensures that the app caters to a broader audience, promoting diversity and usability.

App performance is integral to the user experience. Slow loading times or laggy interactions can frustrate users and lead to abandonment. Optimize app performance by reducing unnecessary animations, optimizing images, and minimizing network requests. Efficient performance contributes to a smoother and more enjoyable UX.

UI/UX design best practices serve as guiding principles for crafting exceptional user experiences in mobile app development. Embracing principles of simplicity, consistency, user-centricity, and accessibility empowers designers to create visually engaging, intuitive, and user-friendly apps. By adhering to these best practices, app developers can enhance user satisfaction, usability, and the overall success of their mobile applications. Effective UI/UX design becomes a powerful tool for capturing user attention, driving engagement, and building lasting relationships with app users in a competitive app landscape.

Creating a Consistent Brand Identity

Establishing a unique and recognizable brand identity is a marketing challenge and a strategic need for success in the rapidly growing mobile app industry. A powerful brand identity extends beyond the app's aesthetic components and captures the spirit of the product, along with its values, character, and the emotional bond it creates with consumers. This section examines the importance of developing a unified brand identity for mobile apps and the fundamental ideas that guide this vital app development process.

The manifestation of an app's distinctive qualities and principles is its brand identity. It encompasses both the way an app shows itself to the outside world and how its users see it. The user experience, messaging, tone of voice, and visual components all work together to communicate this identity. An app with a clear brand identity stands out from the competition, builds user trust, and affects how users see the app.

A strong brand identity is characterized by its visual consistency. It includes all of the visual components that users come into contact with, like the font, color scheme, logo, and images. All touchpoints, including the in-app user interface and the app icon on a user's device, should employ these components consistently. In addition to enhancing brand identification, visual consistency instills user confidence and familiarity.

An app's brand identity is greatly influenced by the language and tone of its messaging. Be it lighthearted, serious, or friendly, the app's tone must always be consistent. The messaging should be consistent with the app's basic ideals and appeal to its intended user base. Users can relate to and interact with a brand with a unified personality developed through consistent tone of voice.

Maintaining a consistent user experience is equally important. The app's design and functionality should reflect the brand's identity and values. By maintaining consistency, users can be guaranteed that their interactions with the app will be logical and predictable. Every element of the app's user experience (UX), including button layout, navigation flow, and general look and feel, should support the brand's identity.

The value proposition and uniqueness of the app are better communicated with a consistent brand identity. It provides a basic response to the query of why users ought to select this app over rivals. A clearly defined brand identity conveys the unique features and advantages that make the app stand out. Users are more inclined to interact with an app and stick with it if they believe it has evident value.

Among users, consistency promotes loyalty and trust. Users gain trust and confidence when they experience a consistent brand identity across all touchpoints. They are more likely to use the app again, interact with it, and refer others to it because they know what to expect from it. Within the app ecosystem, trust is a precious commodity that is based on a consistent brand identity.

While maintaining consistency is essential, a brand's identity should also be adaptable and flexible. Mobile applications are used in ever-changing situations where user preferences, trends, and technology are all changing. A brand's identity must to be flexible enough to change with the times without losing its essence or essential principles. Because of its adaptability, the app will always be relevant and appealing to users with shifting needs.

The long-term success of a mobile app is dependent on maintaining a consistent brand identity, which is an ongoing effort rather than a one-time project. It includes value proposition, user experience, visual consistency, and tone of voice—all supporting user engagement, loyalty, and trust. A strong brand identity sets an app out in a crowded and competitive app market, forges emotional bonds with users, and establishes the foundation for long-term success and growth. An app's lasting impression and its relationship with users are just as crucial to a consistent brand identity as how it appears and functions.

CHAPTER V

Mobile App Development Tools and Technologies

Overview of Development Environments

The creation of mobile apps has become a vital component of contemporary technology, providing many chances for companies and developers to engage with consumers. A development environment provides the framework for building, testing, and releasing applications, and it lies at the heart of every successful mobile application. These development environments include a variety of platforms, frameworks, and tools intended to make the process of creating apps more efficient. We give an overview of development environments in mobile app development in this section, emphasizing their significance and outlining the main choices available to developers.

The digital workshops where the magic of creating apps occurs are called development environments, sometimes called integrated development environments (IDEs). With the tools and resources they provide, developers may quickly bring their ideas to life and reduce the complexity of creating mobile apps. Developers can write, test, and debug code, design user interfaces, manage project resources, and work together in a cohesive workspace that is provided by IDEs. The productivity, code quality, and overall app development experience may all be greatly improved with the correct development environment.

Native development environments are designed for specific mobile platforms, like Android or iOS. They give programmers the ability to design applications that fully use the features of the platform, producing responsive, high-performance, and platform-native user experiences. Apple's Xcode is the primary integrated development environment (IDE) for iOS app development. It provides a range of tools for Objective-C and Swift programming in addition to Interface Builder for UI design. The industry standard for Android development is Android Studio, which offers a powerful environment for developing in Java and Kotlin as well as a graphical designer for creating user interfaces.

Cross-platform app development environments aim to minimize development time and expenses by maximizing code reuse across several platforms. These environments are especially appealing to companies trying to reach a large user base since they allow developers to write code once and deliver it on various devices. The two most well-known cross-platform development environments are Flutter and React Native. Facebook's React Native lets developers create iOS and Android mobile apps with React and JavaScript. Google's Flutter uses the Dart programming language and has many widgets to let you design natively styled user interfaces.

Web technologies such as CSS, HTML, as well as JavaScript are used to create mobile apps in web-based app development environments. These applications, sometimes called Progressive Web Apps (PWAs), can be downloaded and also installed on a user's device or run in a web browser. Programs such as WebStorm and Visual Studio Code offer a lightweight and adaptable programming environment for web-based app development. PWAs are becoming more and more well-liked since they can function like apps on several platforms and in web browsers.

Specialized environments are designed to meet the specific needs of developers and designers of mobile games. When making mobile games, two well-known game development platforms that are frequently used are Unity and Unreal Engine. Unity's user-friendly interface and support for multiple programming languages enable both novice and expert developers to utilize it. The Unreal Engine is preferred for developers who want to make aesthetically spectacular mobile games because of its superior graphics and rendering capabilities.

A new frontier in the development of mobile apps is emerging: cloud-based development environments. These platforms make it convenient to develop, test, and launch programs completely in the cloud, doing away with the requirement for local setups and installations. Platforms such as AWS Cloud9 and Google Cloud Shell provide cloud-based coding environments with integrated development tools, which facilitate quicker collaboration among developers and enable them to access resources from any location with an internet connection.

The foundation of mobile app development is provided by development environments, which provide the resources and tools necessary for developers to produce inventive and user-friendly apps. The target platforms, project specifications, and developer preferences are only a few of the variables that influence the choice of development environment. The choice of development environment can greatly impact the success of a mobile app project, be it native development for platform-specific experiences, cross-platform solutions for code efficiency, web-based approaches for flexibility, or game development environments for immersive experiences. The features and options offered by these development environments will advance along with technology, allowing developers to create mobile apps that push beyond the boundaries of what's feasible.

Choosing a Programming Language

During the process of developing a mobile app, selecting the appropriate programming language is crucial. The programming language is the cornerstone around your app is construction, impacting platform targeting, development time, and app performance. This section examines the important factors to take into account when choosing a programming language for creating mobile applications and goes over a few of the popular languages used in the industry.

The platform you plan to use is one of the most important factors to consider when choosing a programming language. The two main platforms that are used for developing mobile apps are iOS and Android. Whereas Android apps are usually developed with Java or Kotlin, iOS apps are usually developed with Swift or Objective-C. React Native (JavaScript), Flutter (Dart), or Xamarin (C#) are some of the languages and frameworks you can use if you want to make a cross-platform application that runs on iOS and Android. Choose a language that is based on your target audience and project goals, as each has advantages and limitations with regard to compatibility with different platforms.

The rate you can create your app is another important thing to consider. Certain programming languages and frameworks are renowned for their ability to facilitate quick development. For instance, the brief and expressive syntax of languages like Python, Ruby, and JavaScript, for example, makes development more rapid and effective. Comparably, developers can create code only once and have it deployed across several platforms due to cross-platform frameworks like React Native and Flutter, which reduces the development cycle.

A primary issue should be app performance, particularly for resource-intensive apps like games. Languages with strong performance optimization, like Rust, or languages like C++ may be chosen when speed is a top priority. Additionally well-known for their efficiency and capacity to leverage platform-specific features, native languages like Swift and Kotlin are perfect for apps that need to access device features or perform heavy processing.

The quality of the ecosystem and community surrounding a programming language can greatly influence how you develop with it. Robust communities frequently make available enormous libraries, frameworks, and open-source tools that facilitate development and address common problems. Large and vibrant communities exist for popular languages like JavaScript, Python, and Java, making locating resources, tutorials, and support simpler. This assistance can be quite helpful, particularly for those who are just starting out with app development.

Consider the learning curve that comes with the programming language you have selected for your development team and yourself. It could be wise to make use of your team's or your own language proficiency if you or any members of it are already strong. However, if you're just getting started, choose a language with a small learning curve, lots of learning materials, and a thriving development community.

When planning for the future, consider your app's scalability and future-proofing. Choose a programming language that will enable your app to develop and change to meet evolving requirements. Ensure the language can support large-scale apps and won't impede your software's development as it ages.

Selecting a programming language is a crucial decision that can affect your project's outcome while developing a mobile app. Each language has advantages and disadvantages, so you should consider your project's objectives, target platforms, and development team's experience while selecting one. There is a programming language and environment that can suit your demands, regardless of how important cross-platform compatibility, app performance, or development speed are to you. Remember that this is a dynamic choice, and you can decide to utilize several languages and frameworks in a project to take advantage of their specific benefits. Flexibility and agility in language choice can be a great advantage in the fast-paced mobile app development world, helping you make effective and creative apps that cater to your consumers' needs.

Native vs. Cross-Platform Development

The choice between native and cross-platform development is one of the most important ones that mobile app developers must make. This decision greatly impacts the development process, the codebase, performance, user experience, and how resources are allocated. This section examines native and cross- platform development methodologies, going over the important factors that should be taken into account so that developers can make an informed choice.

Developing mobile applications only for a single platform, like iOS or Android, is known as native development. Every platform comes with built-in development environments and native programming languages. While Android apps are written with Java or Kotlin, iOS apps are typically developed with Swift and Objective-C. Native development has a number of benefits.

First of all, native applications offer the best platform optimization. They can fully utilize the device's capabilities and take advantage of platform-specific features. Faster load times and fluid animations are common characteristics of this seamless and responsive user experience. In order to give the app a more native appearance and feel, native development also makes sure that it strictly complies with the platform's design standards.

Second, as compared to their cross-platform equivalents, native apps typically perform better. They can give better speed and responsiveness and are very efficient. This is essential for programs that need to process graphics intensively, communicate with users in real time, or perform resource-intensive tasks.

Native development does, however, present a unique set of difficulties. The requirement to maintain distinct codebases for every platform is a major disadvantage. Longer time to market and more development expenses may result from this. Furthermore, platform-specific languages and tools must be understood by developers, which may call for further training or the recruitment of specialized personnel. Additionally, native development restricts the app's functionality to a single platform, which may exclude a sizable user base.

On the other side, cross-platform development entails developing applications that use a single codebase to run on several platforms. This method's potential for cost savings, code reuse, and quicker development is making it more and more popular. There are several cross- platform frameworks out there, with each having an own set of benefits. These include React Native, Flutter, Xamarin, and PhoneGap.

Code reuse is one of the primary advantages of cross-platform programming. Developers can save their efforts and time by writing code only once and having it deployed across several platforms. This strategy may be very alluring for companies trying to reach a large user base effectively. Because updates and bug fixes can be applied to a single codebase, it also makes maintenance easier.

Various pre-built components and libraries are frequently included in cross-platform frameworks, which facilitates the creation of aesthetically pleasing and consistent user interfaces. In addition to ensuring a consistent look and feel across platforms, this can expedite development.

Cross-platform development is not without its limits, though. Even with high code sharing, platform-specific code or modifications can still be needed to account for differences in user interfaces or device functionality. Because cross-platform apps might not fully utilize the capabilities of each platform, they could also experience performance issues, particularly for tasks requiring a lot of graphics or resources.

The decision between native and cross-platform development ultimately comes down to a number of variables, such as the target audience, project goals, budget, and schedule. Delivering optimal performance and user experience on a single platform is where native development shines. For apps that require optimal speed, make use of platform-specific features, or value a native look and feel, it is frequently the best option.

Cross-platform programming is a desirable alternative for projects with limited resources or strict deadlines since it promotes efficiency and code reuse. It works effectively for apps that need to be released concurrently across several platforms and can offer a wider audience a positive user experience.

Hybrid strategies, like combining cross-platform and native development, can also be effective. Using a cross-platform framework, developers can build a foundational set of capabilities and then add platform-specific functionality or optimizations as needed.

In conclusion, the choice ought to be supported by a thorough evaluation of the needs and goals of the project. It's critical to balance the benefits and drawbacks of both strategies, taking into account elements like long-term maintenance, user experience standards, budget, and development resources. With the right decision between native and cross-platform development, developers can start down a route that leads to a successful mobile app and fits with their project objectives.

Integrating APIs and Third-Party Services

Third-party services and APIs (application programming interfaces) have become essential to developing dynamic, feature-rich mobile applications. By facilitating communication between apps and databases, platforms, and external services, APIs let developers take advantage of a multitude of features without having to create them from scratch. In this section, we examine the importance of incorporating third-party services and APIs into mobile app development, as well as the main advantages and factors to take into account.

Mobile app developers have access to a plethora of opportunities through API connectivity. Rather than building every feature from scratch, developers are able to tap into existing services and resources. This can involve adding payment gateways, mapping services, and cloud storage for improved functionality or integrating social networking platforms for user verification and sharing. Developers may save time and work while offering users a smooth and enhanced experience by utilizing APIs.

The development process is greatly accelerated by integrating APIs. Rather than investing a lot of resources in creating intricate features in-house, developers can rely on well-designed and documented APIs. This reduces the time needed to launch an app and streamlines the development process by allowing developers to concentrate on their primary areas of expertise and delegating specialized work to outside firms.

APIs and third-party services are essential for improving mobile apps' user experiences (UX). Developers may make apps that feel more participatory and intuitive by incorporating services like voice recognition, real-time chat, and geolocation. For example, real-time chat services allow users to communicate instantly within the app, while map integration can give users instructions and location-based recommendations. These qualities enhance the satisfaction and engagement of users.

A multitude of data sources are accessible through APIs, which is beneficial for the functionality of mobile apps. For example, weather applications can use weather APIs to give users forecasts in real time; news apps can use news APIs to get the most recent articles; and e-commerce apps can utilize product catalog APIs to display a variety of products. Access to these data sources keeps app content current and active while enhancing it.

One major benefit of API integration is the abundance of third-party service providers. Because of their dependability and developer-friendly features, well-known platforms like Stripe for payments, Facebook Login, Twitter sharing, and Google Maps are extensively used. Developing seamless integrations of these services into apps is made easier for developers by the abundant documentation, developer communities, and support that these services provide.

Although integrating APIs has many advantages, there are a number of difficulties and things to keep in mind. Since apps must handle user data responsibly while interacting with external services, security and privacy are critical issues. Developers are responsible for making sure that data is transmitted securely and that, when needed, user consent is sought.

The dependability and availability of third-party services can also impact app functionality. Developers should have backup plans ready for situations in which a third-party service goes down or is interrupted.

API integration may also impact an app's performance, particularly if several APIs are accessed at once. Effective resource management and error handling are needed to keep the user experience seamless.

Modern mobile app development requires the core practice of integrating APIs and third-party services. It enables developers to increase the functionality of apps, shorten the time it takes to develop them, and produce more dynamic and engaging user experiences. Although API integration has many benefits, developers should carefully evaluate the implications of API integration for security, dependability, and performance. When used carefully, API integration may be a strong tool for creating innovative, feature-rich mobile apps that meet the wide range of demands and expectations of consumers in the current digital environment.

CHAPTER VI

Building Your Mobile App

Setting Up the Development Environment

Setting up the development environment is one of the crucial first stages before starting the process of creating a mobile app. Coders write, test, and debug code, design user interfaces, and manage project resources in the development environment, often known as the Integrated Development Environment (IDE). It functions as the cornerstone around which the whole process of creating an app is built. This section delves into the importance of configuring the development environment and the essential factors developers need to consider to establish a productive and effective workstation.

One of the most important choices when configuring the development environment is the IDE. The IDE offers an array of tools, code editors, debugging features, and platform and language integration. Other IDE options for mobile app development are catered to certain platforms, such Android Studio for Android and Xcode for iOS. These platform-specific integrated development environments (IDEs) give native app developers a familiar development experience and offer strong integration with their respective ecosystems.

IDEs like Visual Studio Code, JetBrains Rider, and Atom are popular options for cross-platform development. Because of their adaptability and support for a broad variety of programming languages and frameworks, these

IDEs are appropriate for a range of methods in the development of mobile apps. Furthermore, cloud-based coding environments and web-based integrated development environments are becoming more popular, providing the ease of developing from any location with an internet connection.

One of the main components of productive development environments is effective version control. A version control system (VCS) is necessary for developers to monitor code changes, work together as a team, and maintain codebase integrity. Since Git is the most popular version control system and works well with many IDEs, it is a crucial part of the development environment. Development teams can collaborate more effectively and share code by using platforms like GitHub and GitLab, which offer hosting and collaboration options.

Using emulators and simulators in mobile app development is essential since they enable developers to test their applications on virtual devices before releasing them on real smartphones or tablets. IDEs that are cross-platform and platform-specific are also equipped with emulators and simulators that mimic the functionality of actual devices. This helps developers to ensure that the app works and appears as intended across various screen sizes, orientations, and operating system versions by performing extensive testing and debugging.

Configuring project dependencies, application programming interfaces (APIs), and software development kits (SDKs) is another aspect of setting up the development environment. These components allow developers to access third-party services, libraries, and platform-specific capabilities. A plethora of APIs and dependencies are frequently used in mobile app development for activities like authentication, database administration, cloud services, and more. These components' correct configuration and integration are essential for a productive development process.

Continuous integration and continuous deployment, sometimes called CI/CD, is a key component of contemporary mobile app development workflows that automate the build, test, and deployment processes. Code integration, testing, and app store deployment are all automated using CI/CD pipelines that are integrated into the development environment. Jenkins, Travis CI, CircleCI, and other CI/CD systems simplify the development process by cutting down on human labor and facilitating quicker iteration and release cycles.

Setting up the development environment is one of the first steps in developing a mobile app. It creates the workspace where developers test functionality and polish user interfaces while realizing their app concepts. The productivity of development and the quality of the code are greatly impacted by the selection of the IDE, version control system, emulators, and other tools. SDKs, APIs, and dependencies must be configured effectively to access vital resources and services. Adopting CI/CD processes also expedites the deployment of high-quality mobile apps and improves development efficiency.

A properly set development environment is essential for success in today's fast-paced world of app development. Automating difficult and prone to errors processes frees up developers to concentrate on the creative and problem-solving components of app development. By dedicating their time and energy to creating the best possible development environment, developers can start down a path that ends with the creation of successful, entertaining, and user-friendly mobile applications.

Coding Your App

Developing mobile apps process begins with coding, which gives ideas structure and turns them into useful software. It is the process of converting an idea, a design, and a functional specification into computer-readable and executable code. This section examines the value of coding in the creation of mobile apps and the important factors that developers need to consider to produce reliable and effective codebases.

The first important step in coding your app is selecting the right programming language. Your development strategy and target platform will majorly affect the decision. Android apps are typically created in Java or Kotlin, while Swift and Objective-C are frequently used for native iOS development. Languages like JavaScript (with frameworks like React Native), Dart (with Flutter), or C# (with Xamarin) can be used in cross-platform development. Because every language has advantages and disadvantages with different platforms, the choice you choose should be in line with the objectives of your project.

Your app's architecture serves as the roadmap for the coding process. The architectural design outlines the app's structure, including the ways in which data is handled and stored, the user interface is created, and the relationships between different parts. Model-View-Controller (MVC), Model-View-Presenter (MVP), Model-View-ViewModel (MVVM), and Clean Architecture are common architectural patterns in the development of mobile apps. Organization, scalability, and ease of maintenance of the code are all maintained by a well-defined architecture.

A vital component of building a mobile app is designing a UI that is both aesthetically pleasing and easy to use. The user interface (UI) ought to comply with the application's platform-specific norms, user experience standards, and design guidelines. Developers employ UI frameworks and tools to create and customize interface elements like buttons, text fields, navigation bars, and more. Tools for developing responsive and adaptive user interfaces (UIs) that adjust to various screen sizes and orientations are available on platforms like iOS and Android.

Coding entails putting your app's essential features into practice. This includes writing code to manage user interactions, handle data processing, and carry out particular activities. Developers are responsible for ensuring the program functions as intended, whether that involves building complicated business logic, integrating APIs for external services, or developing algorithms for data processing. Finding and fixing any problems or errors in the code requires extensive testing and debugging.

App performance optimization is a continuous effort that starts with code. Memory use, CPU utilization, and network efficiency are some of the things that developers need to be aware of. Caching, background processing, and lazy resource loading are some techniques that help ensure the program stays responsive and effective. Performance optimization is very important for programs that require real-time interactions or are resource-intensive.

A crucial step in the coding process is testing. Tests carried out by developers include unit testing, which evaluates individual code units, integration testing, which examines how multiple components interact, and user testing, which collects input from actual users. Automated testing frameworks and tools facilitate the testing process, guaranteeing that the application operates as intended and is free of serious bugs.

Collaboration between development teams and code maintainability depend on thorough and understandable documentation. Developers should explain the objective of code blocks, functions, and classes through comments, annotations, and documentation. Team members can comprehend and operate with the codebase more easily when well-documented, lowering the learning curve and promoting effective teamwork.

The use of a version control system (VCS), like Git, is essential for teamwork and code management. Developers may save a history of code revisions, track changes, and combine team member contributions with VCS. Development teams may work together more effectively by sharing code and managing projects together due to collaboration technologies like GitHub and GitLab.

The process of turning your idea into a workable program is called coding. Programming languages, architectural design, UI implementation, functionality, performance, testing, documentation, and teamwork must be considered carefully. A successful mobile application relies heavily on its well-crafted codebase, which enhances its usefulness, performance, and maintainability.

To make sure that their code is effective and flexible as the mobile app market changes, developers need to stay current on new trends, technologies, and best practices. As an application develops and grows, coding is a continuous process of improvement and modification rather than a one-time task. By adhering to industry standards for coding and adopting a continuous development philosophy, developers may produce mobile applications that offer exceptional user experiences and endure in a constantly evolving digital landscape.

Testing and Debugging

The unsung heroes of mobile app development are testing and debugging, which discreetly guarantee the quality and reliability of the software that runs our tablets and smartphones. These procedures are essential to producing an app that works as intended and offers a flawless user experience. This section will examine the value of testing and debugging in creating mobile apps, focusing on the essential procedures, resources, and strategies developers use to produce reliable and error- free software.

Testing is, first and foremost, an essential phase in the development lifecycle of mobile apps. It's the methodical assessment of an application's usability, performance, and functionality to find and fix problems. Developers can find and fix bugs with the aid of effective testing, which lowers the possibility of crashes, data loss, and other undesirable outcomes that could harm an app's reputation.

When developing mobile apps, there are several testing methodologies that are each used for a specific reason. For example, unit testing examines individual code units or components to ensure that each one functions as intended. This is a critical procedure that is frequently automated using testing frameworks like as JUnit for Android and XCTest for iOS in order to maintain code correctness. Integration testing evaluates how various app components interact to ensure data flows appropriately and the app functions as a whole.

On the other side, user interface (UI) testing assesses the application's user interface and interaction components. Testers verify for issues including responsiveness, usability, and layout concerns by simulating user interactions with the application. Performance testing evaluates an application's behavior under a variety of scenarios, such as high network traffic or low network connectivity. It assists in locating performance problems, memory leaks, and bottlenecks that could impair user experience.

User Acceptance Testing (UAT), which involves actual users or stakeholders testing the app to make sure it satisfies their needs and expectations, is another crucial testing stage. UAT offers insightful input on functionality, usability, and general user satisfaction, which aids in improving the features and UI of the app.

Debugging is the act of finding, examining, and fixing problems or shortcomings in the application's code; testing and debugging go hand in hand. In addition to being a science, debugging is an art that requires close observation, reasoning, and a little bit of imagination. In order to comprehend the behavior and context of the issue, developers must first recreate it, frequently by following the same processes or conditions that resulted in the problem.

Developers use debugging tools and techniques to determine the root cause of an issue once it has been successfully replicated. Examining error messages, logs, and the flow of code execution may be necessary for this. Developers first identify the issue and then isolate the faulty code or component to reduce the issue's scope. Isolation lowers the chance of adding new bugs by preventing pointless modifications to unaffected areas of the codebase.

Once the problem has been isolated, developers modify the code as needed to resolve it. To make sure the solution addresses the problem without creating any new bugs or side effects, this step calls for thorough testing of the solution. The process of debugging is iterative, meaning that until the problem is entirely resolved, it may take several testing and improvement cycles.

To help them create apps free of bugs, developers use various tools and frameworks in addition to the testing and debugging procedures. While services like Firebase Crashlytics, Fabric, and Microsoft App Center offer real-time crash reporting and analytics for tracking and analyzing app crashes, Xcode Instruments and Android Studio Profilers offer insightful information about app performance.

Additionally, without the requirement for actual devices, developers may recreate and troubleshoot errors on several configurations due to emulators and simulators, which are essential for testing apps on virtual devices. Pipelines for continuous integration and continuous deployment, or CI/CD, automate testing and deployment, facilitating the early detection of problems in the development cycle and guaranteeing the stability of the program through regular updates and releases.

In conclusion, testing and debugging are essential components of developing mobile apps that work together to guarantee the app's dependability, quality, and user experience. Through the use of testing tools and frameworks, debugging techniques, and thorough testing procedures, developers may produce mobile apps that are reliable, dependable, and well-liked by consumers. Throughout an app's lifecycle, testing and debugging are iterative activities that are essential to preserving its dependability and quality in the dynamic mobile market.

Version Control and Collaboration

The foundation of a successful mobile app development project is version control and collaboration, which enables teams to produce high-quality apps, collaborate effectively, and preserve code integrity. This section delves into the importance of version control and collaboration in the creation of mobile apps, examining the essential techniques, resources, and factors that enable developers to optimize their processes and produce outstanding applications.

A methodical way to monitoring and controlling codebase changes during the development process is version control. It enables developers to work together smoothly, record changes, and examine previous iterations of the system. In the world of developing mobile apps, the most popular technology is Git, a distributed version control system. Using Git, developers may establish branches for concurrent development, commit code changes, build repositories, and merge changes back into the main source. Git simplifies issue tracking, promotes collaboration, and guarantees code integrity.

Branching is a fundamental component of version control that enables developers to work on several features or bug fixes at the same time without creating an effect on the main source. GitHub Flow and Gitflow are two branching strategies that specify guidelines for branch creation, merging, and management. Examples of defined branches in Gitflow are "feature," "release," and "hotfix," each with a distinct function. To improve code structure and team coordination, collaborative teams frequently create branching techniques that are customized to their specific development requirements.

Beyond version control, effective cooperation includes platforms and tools that support issue tracking, code reviews, and communication. Git repositories are hosted on platforms like GitHub, GitLab, and Bitbucket, which also provide wikis, pull requests, and issue tracking. These platforms encourage openness by letting team members examine, discuss, and add to code modifications. Procedures for code reviews are essential for preserving code quality, finding errors, and making sure that the code follows best practices.

Code change integration, testing, and deployment are all automated using Continuous Integration and Continuous Deployment, (abbreviated as CI/CD) pipelines. When code changes are posted to the repository, CI/CD solutions like Travis CI, CircleCI, and Jenkins are integrated into version control systems and start automated builds and testing. Through frequent iterations and releases, this automation guarantees that code changes do not cause conflicts or regressions and that the application stays stable and dependable. Development workflows are streamlined by CI/CD pipelines, which enable teams to work quickly without compromising quality.

Code reviews are an essential component of teamwork in creating mobile apps. They give team members the chance to evaluate the quality of the code, spot problems, and exchange information. Adherence to coding standards, constructive criticism, and clear communication are all necessary for successful code reviews. Instead of focusing on criticism, developers should approach code reviews with an eye toward cooperation and improvement. Code quality can be maintained with the help of tools such as linters and code analysis tools, which automatically check for common errors and violations of coding standards.

The thread that holds collaboration together is documentation. Code that is well-documented, README files, and project wikis give team members useful background information and guidance, which facilitates their understanding, utilization, and contribution to the codebase. Apart from code documentation, team meetings, sprint retrospectives, knowledge sharing sessions, and team meetings foster a collaborative and continuous improvement culture.

Collaboration and version control are essential to the accomplishment of mobile app development initiatives. Code management is based on Git and version control systems, which allow teams to work concurrently, preserve code integrity, and methodically track changes. CI/CD pipelines and other collaboration platforms and tools, like GitHub, automate processes, improve communication, and guarantee code quality. A collaborative and knowledge-sharing atmosphere is fostered through documentation, code reviews, and coding standards compliance. Effective version control and collaboration techniques enable development teams to fulfill project deadlines, produce standout mobile apps, and adjust to changing user needs in an industry marked by quick changes and breakthroughs. Adopting these procedures is necessary for app development to be effective and shows how important collaboration and common objectives are to attaining greatness in mobile technology.

CHAPTER VII

Quality Assurance and Testing

Types of Testing (Functional, Usability, Performance)

Testing is a pivotal phase of mobile app development, serving as the bedrock for ensuring that applications meet quality standards, operate as intended, and provide users with outstanding experiences. This testing encompasses a trifecta of vital categories: functional testing, usability testing, and performance testing. Each category plays an indispensable role in the development process, safeguarding mobile app reliability, user-friendliness, and efficiency.

At its core, functional testing revolves around verifying an app's essential functionalities. This testing involves systematically examining every app feature, function, and component to confirm that it operates under predetermined requirements. It calls for creating test cases that encompass a wide array of scenarios, ranging from standard operation to handling edge cases and error scenarios. Functional testing, for example, helps guarantee that users of an e-commerce software can explore products, add products to their shopping carts, finish the checkout process, and receive purchase confirmations without running into critical errors.

Developers employ automated testing frameworks such as XCTest for iOS and Espresso for Android to streamline the functional testing process. These frameworks execute a predefined set of test cases and meticulously compare actual outcomes with anticipated results. Functional testing proves invaluable by uncovering and addressing issues early in the development cycle, guaranteeing the app's dependable functionality and alignment with user expectations.

Usability testing is rooted in the user experience, serving as an evaluative approach to gauge how effectively an app meets the needs and expectations of its intended audience. The focal points here encompass the assessment of the app's user interface (UI), ease of navigation, and overall user experience (UX). Usability testers, often mirroring the app's target user demographic, embark on tasks within the app and offer feedback on its usability, intuitiveness, and user satisfaction.

Usability testing typically encompasses real-world scenarios and user interactions. Testers may be tasked with completing actions like locating specific items in an e-commerce app, registering for an account, or executing a purchase. This approach seeks to identify pain points, spot areas of confusion, and elicit insights into user perceptions and interactions with the app.

Usability testing is a qualitative assessment that synergizes with the quantitative data harnessed from analytics tools. Its purpose lies in refining the app's UI/UX, enhancing its intuitiveness and user-friendliness, which substantially contribute to user retention and overall app triumph.

The final piece in this triad is performance testing, which systematically evaluates an app's performance under various conditions, including heavy loads, challenging network connectivity, and different device configurations. The primary objectives here are to detect bottlenecks, optimize resource utilization, and ensure that the app remains responsive and dependable despite adverse scenarios.

Performance testing embraces diverse dimensions, such as load testing, which assesses an app's performance under a specified number of concurrent users or requests. Stress testing pushes the app beyond its limits to scrutinize its behavior under extreme conditions. Network performance testing simulates diverse network environments, including slow or unreliable connections, to ascertain that the app functions seamlessly. Additionally, resource usage testing keeps tabs on the app's CPU, memory, and battery consumption of system resources.

Performance testing utilities like Apache JMeter, Gatling, and Firebase Performance Monitoring empower developers to execute these tests systematically. Its importance cannot be emphasized because slow or unstable apps frequently cause user frustration and disengagement. Developers can bolster the app's responsiveness and uphold a positive user experience through proactive resolution of performance issues.

In conclusion, functional, usability, and performance testing are the three cornerstones of mobile app development, jointly shaping the foundation for high-quality, user-centric apps. Functional testing verifies the app's essential features, usability testing assesses the user experience, and performance testing guarantees efficiency and reliability under various conditions. Together, these testing types empower developers to craft mobile apps that meet user expectations and thrive in the fiercely competitive app ecosystem. Embracing comprehensive testing strategies across the development lifecycle is not just a best practice but also a testament to the commitment to excellence in mobile app development.

Beta Testing and User Feedback

Beta testing and user feedback are integral to the mobile app development journey, serving as vital tools for refining and perfecting applications. Beta testing, in particular, marks a pivotal phase in the development lifecycle, as it represents the shift from in-house testing to real-world usage. During this phase, a select group of external users, known as beta testers, are given access to a pre-release version of the app, often referred to as the "beta" version. These testers are carefully chosen to represent the app's intended audience, ensuring diverse perspectives and usage scenarios.

The primary objectives of beta testing encompass various dimensions of app improvement. Firstly, beta testers serve as vigilant bug hunters, actively engaging with the app across different devices and operating systems. Their real-world usage uncovers issues and glitches that may have eluded detection during in-house testing. This early bug identification is invaluable for developers, as it allows for prompt resolution and ensures a more stable and reliable final product.

Beyond bug hunting, beta testers evaluate the app's user experience (UX) and user interface (UI). They assess the intuitiveness of the app's navigation, its ease of use, and the overall quality of the user experience. Through their feedback, developers gain insights into areas where the app's design and functionality can be fine-tuned to enhance user satisfaction.

Beta testing also plays a crucial role in identifying compatibility issues. Given the vast array of devices, screen sizes, and network conditions in the mobile landscape, beta testers' usage across various platforms helps pinpoint any compatibility challenges that may arise. By uncovering these issues early on, developers can ensure that the app performs consistently across different configurations, avoiding user frustration.

Moreover, beta testers provide developers with a treasure trove of user insights. They share feature requests, suggestions for enhancements, and feedback on what they appreciate about the app. This user-driven input informs the app's roadmap, helping developers prioritize future updates and align the app more closely with user expectations.

The methodology of beta testing can take different forms. Closed beta testing involves a limited group of pre-selected users invited to participate. This approach offers precise control over the testing group, ensuring that feedback aligns closely with the app's target audience. Open beta testing, on the other hand, opens the beta version to the public, allowing a broader range of users to participate. This approach generates a larger volume of feedback and is often used for apps with a wide user base. Some apps even adopt continuous beta testing, maintaining an ongoing beta program where a dedicated group of beta users tests new features or changes before being released to a broader audience.

In tandem with beta testing, user feedback continues to be a cornerstone of app development. User feedback can be sourced from various channels, including app store reviews, in-app feedback forms, and user surveys. It gives developers direct insights into how users interact with and perceive their apps. This feedback encompasses bug reports, feature requests, usability insights, performance feedback, and positive and negative reviews.

Positive reviews highlight what users find appealing about the app, reinforcing its strengths and features. Negative reviews, while potentially challenging to receive, are invaluable for identifying areas where the app falls short of user expectations. They serve as early warning signals, directing developers' attention to issues that require immediate attention and improvement.

Overall, beta testing and user feedback offer a multitude of benefits. They lead to improved app quality by identifying and rectifying issues, whether technical or usability-related. User feedback enhances user experiences, making apps more user-friendly and satisfying. Moreover, these processes ensure alignment with user preferences and expectations, ultimately increasing user satisfaction and loyalty. They also enable iterative development, allowing apps to evolve and stay competitive in the market. Importantly, beta testing and active solicitation of user feedback demonstrate a commitment to delivering exceptional mobile experiences and fostering user loyalty, both essential for success in today's highly competitive app ecosystem.

Fixing Bugs and Enhancing Stability

In the ever-evolving landscape of mobile app development, ensuring that an application functions smoothly and reliably is paramount. Central to achieving this goal is the process of fixing bugs and enhancing stability. This ongoing endeavor involves identifying, addressing, and preventing issues impacting the app's performance, user experience, and reputation. In this section, we explore the significance of fixing bugs and enhancing stability in mobile app development, detailing the methodologies, challenges, and best practices developers employ to create robust and dependable apps.

Bugs, or software defects, are inherent to the development process. They can manifest in various forms, from critical crashes and functionality glitches to minor annoyances. While some bugs are apparent and easily reproducible, others may lurk beneath the surface, surfacing only under specific conditions or user interactions. Identifying and rectifying bugs is a never-ending task requiring meticulous attention to detail.

The bug-fixing process typically begins with bug reports, which can originate from various sources. Users may report bugs through app store reviews, in-app feedback forms, or customer support channels. Additionally, developers often employ crash reporting tools and error monitoring services that automatically detect and log issues as they occur. These reports provide critical insights into the nature and frequency of bugs.

Not all bugs are created equal, and developers must prioritize which ones to address first. Prioritization hinges on factors such as the bug's severity, its impact on users, and the frequency of occurrence. Critical bugs that lead to app crashes or data loss typically take precedence, as they directly affect the user experience and can result in negative app store reviews or user attrition.

Less severe bugs, such as minor UI glitches or non-essential functionality issues, may be prioritized lower but should not be ignored. A collection of minor bugs can collectively diminish the user experience and tarnish an app's reputation over time. Effective bug tracking and management tools help developers categorize and prioritize issues efficiently.

Fixing bugs is not without its challenges. One common obstacle is the complexity of modern mobile apps, which often involve intricate interactions between multiple components, third-party libraries, and varying device configurations. Identifying the root cause of a bug can be akin to solving a puzzle, requiring a blend of technical expertise, patience, and creative problem-solving.

Another challenge is ensuring that bug fixes do not introduce new issues or regressions. Developers must rigorously test their fixes to verify that they address the problem without unintended side effects. This involves creating test cases replicating the bug's behavior and systematically verifying that the issue is resolved.

Moreover, mobile app development operates within tight release schedules, with pressure to rapidly deliver new features and updates. Balancing bug fixes with feature development is a delicate act, as allocating too much time to bug fixing can impede progress on new features, potentially affecting user engagement and app growth. Effective bug fixing hinges on several best practices. Comprehensive testing is essential to ensure that bug fixes are successful and do not introduce new issues. Unit, integration, and user interface tests are examples of automated testing frameworks that help ensure code accuracy and prevent regressions.

Collaboration among development, testing, and quality assurance teams fosters a culture of bug identification and resolution. Clear communication channels for reporting, tracking, and documenting bugs ensure no issues fall through the cracks.

Version control systems are crucial in managing code changes related to bug fixes. Developers use branching strategies to isolate bug fixes from ongoing development, making applying fixes to the appropriate codebase easier.

Lastly, continuous monitoring and analysis of user feedback and crash reports help developers proactively identify recurring issues and prioritize them for resolution in future updates.

Beyond fixing bugs, enhancing stability involves optimizing an app's performance, reducing memory usage, and minimizing crashes. Resource-hungry components and bottlenecks can be found with the help of performance monitoring tools like crash analytics and app performance profiling. Developers can then apply optimizations to improve the app's responsiveness and efficiency.

Stability enhancements also include thorough regression testing. Developers test the app under various conditions, such as low network connectivity, battery constraints, and different device configurations, to ensure it remains stable and reliable in real-world scenarios.

In conclusion, fixing bugs and enhancing stability are continuous efforts underpinning mobile app development's success. Bugs are a natural part of the development process, and addressing them promptly and effectively is essential for maintaining user satisfaction and app credibility. Developers must prioritize bug fixes based on severity and impact while balancing bug resolution with new feature development. Best practices, collaboration, and comprehensive testing are essential in this endeavor. Enhancing stability goes beyond bug fixing, encompassing performance optimizations and rigorous regression testing to create mobile apps that are not only free of issues but also robust, responsive, and dependable, ensuring a positive user experience and long-term app success.

CHAPTER VIII

App Deployment and Distribution

Preparing Your App for App Stores

As you near the culmination of your mobile app development journey, a critical phase awaits: preparing your app for app stores. This pivotal step bridges the gap between a completed app and its availability to the global audience. This section will explore the significance of app store preparation in mobile app development, detailing the key considerations, guidelines, and best practices developers must follow to ensure a smooth and successful deployment.

Submitting your app to app stores, like the Apple App and Google Play Store, is a multifaceted process that involves several key steps. It begins with ensuring that your app complies with the platform-specific guidelines set by the respective app store.

Platform-specific guidelines are detailed and comprehensive, covering various aspects of app functionality, design, and behavior. These guidelines are designed to maintain a high standard of quality, security, and user experience across all apps in the store. Deviating from these guidelines can result in app rejection or removal, requiring developers to review and adhere to them thoroughly.

Rigorous quality assurance and testing are essential before submitting your app to an app store. This encompasses identifying and resolving bugs and ensuring that the app functions smoothly across various devices, screen sizes, and operating system versions. Comprehensive testing, including manual and automated testing, should be carried out to validate that the app meets the platform's performance and stability requirements.

Moreover, usability testing is crucial to confirm that the user interface and user experience align with best practices and user expectations. Usability issues, if not addressed, can result in a poor user rating and user churn after the app is deployed.

In addition to the app itself, developers must prepare a range of assets and metadata for the app store submission. This includes creating visually appealing and informative app store listings that entice potential users to download the app. High-quality app icons, screenshots, and promotional images should be crafted to showcase the app's features and benefits.

Crafting an engaging and concise app description is equally important. The app description should effectively communicate the app's value proposition, features, and functionalities to potential users. Developers should also select appropriate keywords and categories to optimize the app's discoverability within the app store.

App stores have strict policies to ensure their ecosystems' safety and security. Developers must thoroughly review and adhere to these policies, covering privacy, data handling, and security measures. For instance, privacy policies are essential for apps that collect user data, and developers must provide clear and transparent explanations of data usage practices.

Understanding and complying with these policies is a prerequisite for app store submission and a commitment to safeguarding user trust and data integrity. Failure to comply can result in app removal and damage to the developer's reputation.

Once all the prerequisites are met, the app store submission process can begin. This typically involves creating developer accounts on the respective app stores, completing submission forms, and providing the necessary assets and metadata. Submission forms may require app name, description, pricing, and contact information.

After submission, the app undergoes a review process conducted by the app store's team. This review assesses the app's compliance with guidelines, functionality, and overall quality. The review process duration varies depending on the app store, ranging from a few days to several weeks.

While waiting for app store approval, developers should prepare for the app's launch. This includes planning marketing strategies, notifying potential users, and establishing a support channel for user inquiries and feedback.

After approval, the app is then released to the app store, where it can be downloaded by anyone in the world. Developers must actively monitor user reviews, address issues promptly, and continuously work on app updates to enhance user experience and maintain a positive app store rating.

In conclusion, preparing your app for app stores is a pivotal phase in mobile app development that involves careful adherence to platform-specific guidelines,

rigorous testing, and meticulous attention to detail. It is not only a culmination of development efforts but also the commencement of a new phase where your app has the potential to reach millions of users worldwide. Adhering to app store policies, creating engaging app store listings, and fostering a commitment to quality are key factors in ensuring a successful deployment. Ultimately, the app store submission process is a testament to your dedication to delivering exceptional mobile experiences and a stepping stone to realizing your app's potential in
the digital marketplace.

Submitting Your App to App Stores

Submitting your app to app stores marks a pivotal milestone in the mobile app development journey. It represents the moment when your hard work and creativity become accessible to a global audience. However, this process is not as simple as hitting the "submit" button. It involves careful planning, adherence to platform-specific guidelines, and a strategic approach to ensure your app's success in the competitive app marketplace. This section will delve into the significance of submitting your app to app stores, outlining the key considerations, challenges, and best practices developers must navigate to achieve a smooth and successful deployment.

One of the first and most critical considerations when submitting your app to app stores is compliance with platform-specific guidelines. Both Apple's App and Google's Play Store have stringent guidelines in place to maintain a high standard of quality, security, and user experience for their users. Deviating from these guidelines can result in your app being either rejected or removed from the store, making it imperative for developers to review and adhere to them thoroughly.

Platform-specific guidelines encompass various aspects of app functionality, design, and behavior. They cover everything from user interface design and data privacy to payment processing and content restrictions. Developers must ensure that their app aligns with these guidelines before submitting it for review.

Before submission, rigorous quality assurance and testing are essential. This process goes beyond identifying and fixing bugs, although it is a crucial part. Comprehensive testing, including manual and automated testing, should be carried out to validate that the app meets the platform's performance and stability requirements.

Furthermore, usability testing is crucial to confirm that the user interface and user experience align with best practices and user expectations. Usability issues, if not addressed, can result in a poor user rating and user churn after the app is deployed.

In addition to the app itself, developers must prepare a range of assets and metadata for the app store submission. These elements are instrumental in presenting your app to potential users and enticing them to download it. High-quality assets, such as app icons, screenshots, and promotional images, should be carefully crafted to effectively showcase the app's features and benefits.

Crafting an engaging and concise app description is equally important. The app description should effectively communicate the app's value proposition, features, and functionalities to potential users. Developers should also select appropriate keywords and categories to optimize the app's discoverability within the app store.

App stores have strict policies to ensure their ecosystems' safety and security. Developers must thoroughly review and adhere to these policies, covering areas such as privacy, data handling, and security measures. For instance, privacy policies are essential for apps that collect user data, and developers must provide clear and transparent explanations of data usage practices.

Understanding and complying with these policies is a prerequisite for app store submission and a commitment to safeguarding user trust and data integrity. Failure to comply can result in app removal and damage to the developer's reputation.

Once all prerequisites are met, the app store submission process can commence. This typically involves creating developer accounts on the respective app stores, completing submission forms, and providing the necessary assets and metadata. Submission forms may require details such as app name, description, pricing, and contact information.

After submission, the app undergoes a review process conducted by the app store's team. This review assesses the app's compliance with guidelines, functionality, and overall quality. The review process duration varies depending on the app store, ranging from a few days to several weeks.

While awaiting app store approval, developers should actively prepare for the app's launch. This includes planning marketing strategies, notifying potential users, and establishing a support channel for user inquiries and feedback.

After approval, the app is then released to the app store, where it can be downloaded by anyone in the world. Developers must proactively monitor user reviews, address issues promptly, and continuously work on app updates to enhance user experience and maintain a positive app store rating.

In conclusion, submitting your app to app stores is a multifaceted and strategic process requiring meticulous planning, guidelines adherence, and a commitment to quality. It is not only the culmination of development efforts but also the commencement of a new phase where your app has the potential to reach millions of users worldwide. Adhering to app store policies, creating engaging app store listings, and fostering a dedication to quality are key factors in ensuring a successful deployment. Ultimately, the app store submission process is a testament to your dedication to delivering exceptional mobile experiences and a stepping stone to the realization of your app's potential in the digital marketplace.

App Store Optimization (ASO)

It can be quite difficult to stand out from the competition and make sure your app reaches the target audience in the ever-expanding world of mobile apps. App Store Optimization, or ASO, is useful in this situation. ASO is a multifaceted strategy that involves optimizing various elements of your app's presence on app stores to enhance its discoverability, visibility, and appeal to potential users. In this section, we will delve into the significance of App Store Optimization, outlining the key components, techniques, and best practices that can propel your app towards success in the competitive app marketplace.

Visibility is paramount in the vast and ever-growing catalog of apps available on platforms like the Apple App Store and Google Play Store. Users typically discover and explore new apps through app store searches, recommendations, and rankings. ASO is the set of tactics employed to maximize your app's presence in these crucial discovery channels.

One of the core components of ASO is keyword optimization. It involves selecting relevant keywords and phrases that potential users might use when searching for apps similar to yours. These keywords should be strategically incorporated into your app's title, description, and metadata. Thorough research and analysis of popular and competitive keywords are essential to ensure your app appears in relevant search results.

Your app's title and description are often the first things potential users see. They should be concise, descriptive, and compelling. A well-crafted title should convey the app's purpose and value proposition succinctly. The description should provide additional context, highlighting key features and benefits. Using persuasive language and calls to action can also entice users to download your app.

Visual elements play a crucial role in ASO. Your app icon, screenshots, and promotional images should be of high quality and visually appealing. They should effectively convey the app's core features and user experience. Striking visuals can capture the attention of potential users and encourage them to explore your app further. The visibility and legitimacy of an app are greatly impacted by user ratings and reviews. Getting pleased users to rate and review your app will help it become more well-known. Responding to negative feedbacks in a timely and helpful manner shows that you value customer feedback and gives you the chance to make improvements to your app.

Localization is a valuable ASO strategy if your target audience spans multiple regions and languages. Translating your app's title, description, and keywords into numerous languages can broaden your app's global reach. It's essential to consider regional preferences and cultural nuances when localizing your app's content.

ASO is a continuous process rather than a one-time endeavor. Regularly monitoring your app's performance on app stores, tracking keyword rankings, and analyzing user feedback are essential. ASO is dynamic, and adjustments may be necessary to adapt to changes in user behavior, competition, or platform algorithms.

While ASO offers a multitude of benefits, it comes with its challenges. The app marketplace is highly competitive, with millions of apps vying for attention. Staying up to date with ever-evolving algorithms and guidelines on different platforms can be daunting. Additionally, achieving the right balance between keyword optimization and maintaining a user-friendly and engaging app store listing requires careful consideration.

In today's fiercely competitive app marketplace, App Store Optimization (ASO) is the linchpin that can elevate your app's discoverability and success. ASO encompasses keyword optimization, compelling app titles and descriptions, high-quality visuals, user ratings and reviews, localization, and continuous monitoring and iteration. It's not a one-time effort but a dynamic and ongoing process that requires dedication and strategic thinking.

By implementing ASO best practices, you can improve your app's visibility in app store searches, attract more users, and ultimately increase your app's chances of success. ASO empowers you to connect with your target audience, make a positive impression, and stand out in the crowded app landscape. It's a crucial tool for any app developer looking to make their mark in the digital realm.

Launch Strategies and Marketing

After months of development and meticulous planning, the day of your app's launch is finally on the horizon. However, a successful launch is not guaranteed in the dynamic and competitive world of mobile apps. This is where launch strategies and marketing come into play. Effectively introducing your app to the world, generating initial user interest, and building momentum are essential for a strong start and long-term success. This section will explore the significance of launch strategies and marketing in mobile app development, outlining key components, best practices, and insights to help you navigate this crucial phase.

Before diving into marketing strategies, thorough pre-launch preparation is essential. This phase includes finalizing your app's features, design, and functionality, conducting comprehensive testing to iron out any remaining bugs, and ensuring that your app complies with all app store guidelines. Crafting compelling app store assets, such as an engaging app description, high-quality screenshots, and an eye-catching app icon, is crucial. These assets are potential users' first impressions of your app and can significantly influence their decision to download it.

Understanding your app's target audience is foundational to your marketing strategy. Who are your ideal users? What problems does your app solve for them? What demographics, interests, and behaviors define your audience? The more specific and detailed your understanding of your target users, the better you can tailor your marketing efforts to reach them effectively.

As mentioned earlier, App Store Optimization (ASO) is a critical component of your marketing strategy. ASO involves optimizing your app's visibility and discoverability in app stores. This includes selecting relevant keywords, crafting an attention-grabbing app title and description, and creating visually appealing app store assets. A well-optimized app store listing can significantly increase your app's chances of being found by potential users.

Creating a web presence for your app is another crucial step. This includes setting up a dedicated website or landing page that provides information about your app, its features, and its benefits. You can use this platform to engage with potential users, share updates, and collect email addresses for future communication.

App marketers have access to effective tools on social media networks. Make a name for yourself on channels that appeal to your intended market and produce engaging content that highlights the positive features of your app. To reach a larger audience and encourage app downloads, think about launching paid advertising campaigns on social media platforms including Facebook, Instagram, and also Twitter.

Content marketing is the process of producing and disseminating informative content about the market or specialty of your app. This can include blog posts, articles, videos, or podcasts that educate, inform, or entertain your target audience. By providing valuable content, you can build credibility, attract an audience interested in your app's niche, and direct them to your app.

Collaborating with influencers who have a following in your app's niche can be a potent marketing strategy. Influencers can provide authentic reviews and endorsements, engaging their audience with your app's message. However, choosing influencers whose values and audience align with your app is crucial.

Some app stores offer promotional opportunities for new apps. These can include featuring your app in curated lists, banners, or special sections. Applying for these features can increase your app's visibility and downloads significantly.

After your app's launch, engagement with your users becomes paramount. Respond promptly to user feedback and reviews, addressing issues and continuously improving your app. Update your app regularly with fresh features and improvements to keep customers interested and devoted. Engaging with your user community through social media and email newsletters helps maintain interest and foster a sense of community around your app.

In conclusion, launch strategies and marketing are pivotal in the mobile app development journey. A successful launch involves meticulous pre-launch preparation, understanding your target audience, optimizing your app store presence, and leveraging various marketing channels and techniques. Building a web presence, social media engagement, content marketing, influencer collaborations, and app store promotions all contribute to a robust marketing strategy. However, the work continues after launch; post-launch engagement and continuous improvement are essential for sustaining and growing your app's user base. Effective marketing drives initial downloads and establishes a foundation for long-term app success in a competitive and dynamic landscape.

CHAPTER IX

Post-Launch Activities

Monitoring User Feedback and Analytics

In the realm of mobile app development, the journey continues after a successful launch. Once your app is in the hands of users, the real work begins: monitoring user feedback and analytics. This ongoing process is instrumental in understanding how your app is performing, identifying areas for improvement, and making data driven decisions to enhance user satisfaction and app success. In this section, we'll delve into the significance of monitoring user feedback and analytics in mobile app development, exploring key components, best practices, and the invaluable insights that can be acquired from this process.

User feedback is a treasure trove of insights that can inform your app's development and evolution. It encompasses various inputs, including app store reviews, in-app feedback forms, customer support inquiries, and user surveys. Each piece of feedback provides a glimpse into the user experience, highlighting strengths and improvement areas.

Reviews on the app store, in particular, provide a public forum for users to express their ideas and opinions. Positive reviews reinforce what users love about your app, serving as a testament to your app's strengths. Negative reviews, while potentially challenging to receive, pinpoint specific pain points and issues that require attention.

In-app feedback forms and customer support inquiries offer a direct channel for users to voice their concerns or report problems. These channels enable you to gather feedback from users who may not leave app store reviews, helping you address issues and improve the user experience.

In addition to user feedback, user analytics provide quantitative insights into how users engage with your app. Analytical tools track user behaviors, such as app usage patterns, session durations, feature engagement, and more. These metrics offer a comprehensive view of user interactions and can reveal usage trends and bottlenecks within your app.

For instance, user analytics can show you which features are most popular and which are rarely used. They can also highlight drop-off points in the user journey, indicating where users may encounter difficulties or abandon the app. With this data, you can prioritize enhancements and optimize the user experience accordingly.

Mobile app development is iterative by nature, and monitoring user feedback and analytics fuels this improvement cycle. Regularly reviewing and acting upon user feedback and analytics enables you to create informed decisions about feature enhancements, bug fixes, and usability improvements.

User feedback can be categorized and prioritized based on severity and impact. Critical issues, such as app crashes or data loss, should be addressed promptly to ensure the app's stability and reliability. Usability and feature requests can be grouped and considered for future updates.

User analytics can inform feature development by revealing user preferences and behaviors. For example, if analytics show that a particular feature is underutilized, it may be worth revisiting its design or considering whether it aligns with user needs.

Monitoring user feedback and analytics is not a one-time task but an ongoing commitment to app improvement. Regularly scheduled reviews of user feedback and analytics help you stay attuned to user sentiment and app performance. Implementing changes based on these insights demonstrates your commitment to delivering an exceptional user experience.

Moreover, continuous enhancement keeps your app competitive in a dynamic landscape. As user expectations evolve and new technologies emerge, your app must adapt to remain relevant and appealing.

User feedback and analytics should be central in shaping your app's roadmap. Feedback and data-driven insights can help you prioritize new features, enhancements, and bug fixes. Maintaining a feedback loop with your development team is essential to ensure that user insights are integrated into development decisions.

Monitoring user feedback and analytics is a fundamental practice in mobile app development. User feedback offers qualitative insights into the user experience, highlighting strengths and improvement areas. User analytics provide quantitative data on user behavior and app usage patterns. By consistently reviewing and acting upon this feedback and data, you can iteratively enhance your app, making it more user-friendly, reliable, and competitive in the app marketplace. This commitment to improvement fosters user satisfaction and loyalty and positions your app for long-term success in an ever-evolving digital landscape.

Continuous Improvement and Updates

A finished product is a bit of a misconception in the fast-paced world of mobile app development. In reality, an app's release marks just the beginning of its journey. To thrive and remain competitive, apps must embrace a culture of continuous improvement and updates. This involves ongoing refinement, feature enhancements, and bug fixes to address user feedback and evolving market trends. In this section, we'll explore the significance of continuous improvement and updates in mobile app development, outlining the key components, best practices, and the enduring value they bring to developers and users.

Understanding the lifecycle of a mobile app is crucial to grasping the importance of continuous improvement. It typically comprises several phases: ideation, development, testing, launch, and post-launch. However, constant improvement and updates take center stage in the post-launch phase.

Once your app is in the hands of users, it becomes a dynamic entity subject to user feedback, changing user preferences, evolving technologies, and competition. Failing to recognize this reality and neglecting to make necessary updates can lead to stagnation and declining user satisfaction.

User feedback is a potent source of insight and a catalyst for improvement. It's the voice of your users, offering invaluable input on their experiences, needs, and pain points. Developers should actively encourage users to provide feedback through in-app feedback forms, app store reviews, and customer support channels.

Negative feedback highlights areas requiring immediate attention, such as bug fixes or usability improvements. Positive feedback and feature requests offer opportunities for enhancement and expansion. By showing that you are dedicated to your users' satisfaction, you may establish a partnership and earn their trust by paying attention to their input and acting upon it.

Iterative development concepts are the foundation of ongoing upgrades and enhancements. Developers use an agile methodology instead of aiming for a flawless, feature-rich app at launch. They make available an MVP (minimum viable product) in order to get input from users and make adjustments depending on actual usage. Iterative development allows developers to refine and enhance the app over time, aligning it more closely with user expectations and needs. It also mitigates the risk of spending excessive resources on features that may not resonate with users.

One of the primary reasons for continuous updates is the identification and resolution of bugs and performance issues. No matter how rigorous the testing phase, real-world usage can uncover unexpected problems. Promptly addressing these issues is essential to maintaining app stability and user trust.

Performance optimization is another vital aspect of updates. As new devices and operating system versions emerge, optimizing your app to ensure it runs smoothly on the latest hardware and software is crucial. Apps should be quick to respond to user requests and efficient; otherwise, users may stop using the app.

Improvements to features are a major factor in upgrades. Consumers value apps that adapt to better meet their demands. It is possible to find opportunities for new feature introduction, feature simplification, or feature extension by analyzing user behavior and comments.

Enhancements to features keep current users engaged as well as draw in new ones. If a software continuously adds new features and makes improvements, users are more inclined to stay with it. It's essential to balance addressing existing issues and introducing exciting new features.

In the ever-evolving app marketplace, staying competitive is a continuous challenge. New entrants and existing competitors continually innovate and update their apps to meet user demands. To remain relevant and competitive, your app must evolve in response to changing market dynamics.

Continuous updates are an essential part of your app's competitive strategy. Regularly assessing user expectations and industry trends allows you to make strategic updates that keep your app ahead of the curve.

Effective communication with your user base is pivotal during the update process. Notify users of updates through app store release notes and in-app messages. Clearly articulate the benefits and improvements introduced in each update. Engage with users through social media, email newsletters, and feedback channels to keep them informed and involved in your app's journey.

Continuous improvement and updates are not mere maintenance tasks but a testament to your commitment to user satisfaction and app excellence. They represent a dynamic approach to mobile app development, acknowledging that an app's journey is lifelong. Addressing user feedback, iterative development, bug fixes, performance optimization, and feature enhancements all contribute to a vibrant, engaging, and competitive app. Embracing continuous improvement ensures that your app remains a valuable asset to users and a relevant player in the ever-evolving landscape of mobile technology.

Handling User Support and Feedback

In the world of mobile app development, user support and feedback play a pivotal role in shaping the success and longevity of an application. Effective handling of user inquiries, concerns, and suggestions fosters trust and loyalty and provides developers with invaluable insights to continually enhance their apps. This section will explore the significance of handling user support and feedback in mobile app development, outlining key components, best practices, and the mutual benefits for developers and users.

A user-centric approach is at the heart of successful app development. Acknowledging that users are the lifeblood of an app's success, developers must prioritize their needs and experiences. User support and feedback mechanisms are the conduits through which developers can engage directly with their user base, gaining a deep understanding of their expectations and challenges.

User support and feedback channels are multifaceted, encompassing various touchpoints where users can contact developers and provide input. These channels include in-app feedback forms, customer support emails, social media platforms, app store reviews, and user surveys.

In-app feedback forms are essential for capturing user sentiments and issues directly within the app. They provide users with a convenient means to report problems, request assistance, or share feedback while their experience with the app is fresh in their minds.

Customer support emails offer users a more personalized and direct communication channel. Users encountering critical issues or requiring specific assistance often turn to this channel for prompt and tailored responses.
Social media platforms offer a broader stage for user interactions. Engaging with users through social media allows developers to showcase their responsiveness, address concerns publicly, and build a sense of community around the app.

App store reviews serve as a public forum where users can express their opinions, offer suggestions, and rate their app experience. Positive and negative reviews give developers valuable insights into what users appreciate and where improvements are needed.

User surveys, whether conducted within the app or through other channels, provide a structured way to collect user feedback on specific aspects of the app, such as usability, feature preferences, or overall satisfaction.

User feedback serves as a compass guiding app development in the right direction. Negative feedback highlights critical issues that require immediate attention, such as bug fixes or usability improvements. Addressing these issues demonstrates responsiveness and a commitment to user satisfaction.

Positive feedback and feature requests offer opportunities for enhancement and expansion. Users often provide valuable suggestions for improving the app or introducing new capabilities. Engaging with users and implementing their suggestions enhances the app and strengthens the developer-user relationship.

Efficient handling of user support and feedback builds trust and loyalty among your user base. Users appreciate when their concerns are heard, and their problems are resolved promptly and effectively. A positive support experience can turn a dissatisfied user into a loyal advocate for your app.

Consistent communication, transparent updates, and active engagement on social media further solidify trust and loyalty. When users feel heard and respected, they are more willing to promote and use the app in the future.

User feedback serves as a continuous source of improvement. It fuels an iterative development process, where developers regularly assess user input and make data-driven decisions to enhance the app's performance, usability, and overall user experience.

By embracing a cycle of feedback, evaluation, and action, developers ensure that their app evolves in step with changing user expectations and technological advancements. This iterative approach sustains the app's relevance and positions it for long-term success.

Handling user support and feedback is a cornerstone of mobile app development that benefits developers and users. It fosters a user-centric approach, builds trust and loyalty, and provides insights for continuous improvement. Developers should actively engage with their user base through various channels, respond promptly and effectively to user inquiries and concerns, and continually implement user feedback to enhance their apps. In this reciprocal relationship, developers empower users to be active contributors to the app's evolution, ensuring its ongoing relevance and success in the dynamic world of mobile technology.

Scaling Your App

In mobile app development, scaling an app represents a crucial phase in its journey towards becoming a thriving digital entity. This process involves expanding an app's capacity, functionality, and user base to meet increased popularity demands and seize new opportunities. The significance of scaling your app cannot be overstated, as it paves the way for sustained growth and competitiveness.

Understanding app scaling is fundamental. It can manifest in various ways, such as accommodating a growing user base, handling increased data volumes, expanding feature sets, or reaching new geographic markets. Each dimension of scaling presents unique challenges and requires strategic planning.

Infrastructure scaling is often the starting point. Whether scaling horizontally by adding more servers or vertically by upgrading existing resources, having a scalable infrastructure is crucial. Platforms for cloud computing such as Google Cloud, Microsoft Azure, and AWS (Amazon Web Services) provide adaptable solutions that may adapt to meet your app's changing needs.

Database scalability is another critical consideration, primarily if your app deals with substantial amounts of data. Approaches like sharding (partitioning data across multiple databases) or using NoSQL databases designed for high scalability can help manage data growth effectively.

Optimized code and architecture are foundational elements of scalability. Efficient, well-structured code minimizes resource usage and enhances performance. Adopting microservices or modular architecture can facilitate independent scaling of specific components within your app.

Load balancing and caching are vital to distributing incoming traffic across multiple servers and reducing server load. These mechanisms improve response times and overall scalability.

Continuous monitoring and analytics are indispensable for identifying performance bottlenecks and areas requiring scaling. Tools like New Relic, Datadog, or Google Analytics provide real-time insights into app performance and user behavior.

Security and compliance must be noticed during scaling. As your app grows, safeguarding user data and adhering to regulatory requirements, such as GDPR, are critical considerations. Implementing robust security measures becomes increasingly important.

Maintaining a seamless user experience is paramount during scaling. Users should not experience disruptions or performance degradation as your app expands. Furthermore, scalability should not hinder your ability to provide efficient user support and handle inquiries effectively.

Comprehensive testing, including load testing and performance testing, is essential to identify and address potential issues. A controlled testing environment ensures a smooth transition during the scaling process.

Scalability planning is the foundation for effective scaling. This involves anticipating future growth and challenges. Key aspects include developing a scalability roadmap, resource allocation, redundancy and failover planning, and cost management.

In conclusion, scaling your app is a transformative journey that requires meticulous planning, infrastructure optimization, and an unwavering commitment to ongoing improvement. Scalability is the linchpin for sustaining a seamless user experience, seizing new opportunities, and maintaining competitiveness. By embracing infrastructure scalability, database efficiency, optimized code, load balancing, monitoring, security measures, and comprehensive testing, you position your app for success in the dynamic landscape of mobile app development.

CHAPTER X

Legal and Ethical Considerations

Intellectual Property Rights

In the dynamic realm of mobile application development, intellectual property (IP) rights are essential for safeguarding the innovative products of creativity. As developers design and build new apps, they generate intellectual property encompassing a spectrum of rights, including copyright, trademarks, patents, and trade secrets. Understanding and safeguarding these rights is essential for fostering innovation, ensuring fair competition, and reaping the rewards of ingenuity.

Copyright, one of the fundamental IP rights, protects original works of authorship, such as app code, design elements, graphics, music, and literary content. In mobile app development, copyright applies to the source code, user interfaces, and any original content within the app. It grants the developer exclusive rights to reproduce, distribute, and display their work.

Trademarks safeguard distinctive symbols, logos, names, and branding elements associated with an app. A strong trademark protects a developer's brand identity and prevents others from using similar branding that could confuse consumers.

Patents protect novel and non-obvious inventions. This could include unique algorithms, processes, or functionalities that offer a significant technical advantage in the app world. Patents provide exclusive rights to use, make, or sell the patented invention.

Trade secrets encompass confidential information, such as proprietary algorithms, formulas, or techniques that give an app a competitive edge. Protecting trade secrets involves maintaining their confidentiality within the development team and through legal agreements.

The importance of intellectual property rights in mobile app development cannot be overstated. First and foremost, they protect developers from unauthorized use or replication of their work. This protection extends to the prevention of others copying app features, branding, or functionalities without permission.

Additionally, intellectual property rights encourage developers to devote their time, resources, and ingenuity to the creation of apps. Developers are more willing to experiment and push the limits of what is feasible in the field of mobile app development when they are aware that their creations are protected.

IP rights can also confer a significant market advantage. Securing these rights allows developers to differentiate their app, establish a unique brand identity, and license their technology to others. In essence, IP rights become a strategic asset.

Monetization is another aspect of IP rights that developers can explore. By licensing their intellectual property through agreements, developers can generate revenue by granting others permission to use or integrate their IP into their products.

Best practices for protecting intellectual property in mobile app development encompass several key principles. First, documenting everything related to app development is crucial. Detailed records of code revisions, design iterations, and any innovations serve as valuable evidence of IP rights.

Contracts play a pivotal role in IP protection. When collaborating with others, well-defined contracts delineating ownership and usage rights for the app's IP are essential. Non-disclosure agreements (NDAs) can also help protect trade secrets when sharing sensitive information with third parties.

Registering IP with the relevant government authorities is a proactive step developers can take to strengthen their legal standing in case of disputes. Copyrights, trademarks, and patents can all benefit from official registration.

Developers should also review third-party assets used in their apps, such as libraries or open-source code, to ensure proper licensing and compliance with terms. Educating the development team about the importance of IP rights and the need to respect and protect them is equally essential.

Finally, enforcing IP rights is a crucial aspect of protection. In case of suspected infringements, developers should consult with legal professionals to take appropriate action, including sending cease-and-desist letters or pursuing legal remedies.

Mobile app development introduces unique challenges for protecting intellectual property. The industry's fast-paced nature, the prevalence of open-source software, and the global reach of apps add complexity to IP protection.

Moreover, the line between inspiration and infringement can sometimes be blurry, requiring developers to navigate this terrain carefully to avoid unintentional IP violations while drawing inspiration from existing apps and technologies.

In conclusion, intellectual property rights are the bedrock of innovation and fair competition in mobile app development. They provide developers with the legal framework to protect their creative efforts, incentivize innovation, and capitalize on their ingenuity. App developers can secure their place in the dynamic and evolving landscape of mobile technology by understanding the types of IP rights, adopting best practices for protection, and staying vigilant in enforcing their rights.

Privacy and Data Security

In the digital age, where mobile apps have become integral to our daily lives, privacy and data security have emerged as paramount concerns. Mobile app developers entrusted with access to users' personal information must prioritize protecting this sensitive data to earn and maintain user trust. Privacy breaches and data mishandling can have severe consequences, ranging from legal penalties to reputational damage. In this section, we will explore the significance of privacy and data security in mobile app development, highlighting key considerations, best practices, and their profound impact on user trust and app success.

User trust is the lifeblood of mobile app success. Users willingly share personal information when they download and use apps, from email addresses to location data and payment details. In return, they expect developers to treat their data carefully and respect their privacy.

Respecting this expectation is required by law as well as morality. Strict guidelines govern the collection, storage, and processing of user data. Examples of these regulations are the California Consumer Privacy Act, also known as the CCPA, in the United States and the GDPR, which stands for the General Data Protection Regulation, in Europe. Serious fines and legal repercussions could result from noncompliance.

Key Considerations for Privacy and Data Security include data minimization (collect only necessary data), consent and transparency (clearly communicate data usage), data encryption (protect data in transit and at rest), access control (restrict data access), data retention policies, security testing, vetting third-party providers, and developing an incident response plan.

Best privacy and data security practices involve privacy by design, regular updates, secure authentication, secure communication, data backups, security training, and privacy impact assessments.

When developers prioritize privacy and data security, they signal their commitment to user trust and protection. An app that shows a strong commitment to protecting user data is more likely to be used by users. On the other hand, apps with a history of privacy incidents or data breaches often face user backlash and may struggle to regain trust.

Maintaining user trust through robust privacy and data security measures is ethical and a competitive advantage. Users are more likely to choose and stick with apps that respect their privacy, protect their data, and adhere to the highest standards of security.

In conclusion, privacy and data security are non-negotiable elements of mobile app development in the digital age. They are not just legal requirements but essential components of user trust and app success. Developers must adopt a privacy-first mindset, implement robust security measures, and stay vigilant against emerging threats. By doing so, they not only protect their users but also build a strong foundation for the long-term success of their apps in an increasingly data-conscious world.

Compliance with App Store Guidelines

When developing a mobile app, publishing it to app stores is frequently the first step towards getting your creation in front of people. The Apple App, Google Play Store, and other platforms act as gatekeepers, making sure that programs adhere to strict requirements and restrictions prior to being made accessible to the general public. Following these recommendations is crucial to getting your app approved, keeping up a good reputation, and guaranteeing long-term success.

Compliance with app store guidelines is the first step toward making your app accessible to a wide user base. These guidelines are designed to maintain quality, security, and consistency within the app store ecosystems. They aim to protect users from potential harm, such as malicious software or subpar user experiences. By adhering to these guidelines, developers increase their chances of getting their apps approved and signal their commitment to user satisfaction and data security.

Key considerations for app store compliance encompass several critical aspects. Platform-specific guidelines are fundamental, as each app store has its own rules and policies that developers must adhere to. Understanding these guidelines is essential to avoid common pitfalls and ensure your app meets platform-specific requirements.

User privacy is central to app store guidelines. Developers must be transparent about data collection, inform users how their data will be used, and obtain clear consent when necessary. This aligns with global data protection regulations like GDPR and CCPA.

App functionality must align with the guidelines. This includes avoiding deceptive behavior, ensuring that the app works as intended, and preventing excessive bugs or crashes that could compromise the user experience. When it comes to app store compliance, security measures are crucial. The implementation of strong security measures and adherence to encryption standards are necessary for developers in order to safeguard user data against vulnerabilities.

Content guidelines are also significant, encompassing restrictions on explicit or harmful content, copyright infringement, and hate speech. Adhering to these guidelines ensures that the app's content aligns with the store's policies.

Best practices for app store compliance involve a proactive approach. Before submitting your app, conduct a thorough review to ensure it aligns with the platform-specific guidelines and policies. Address any potential issues proactively. Prioritize user-centric design and ensure that your app provides value to users while respecting their privacy. Transparently communicate data collection practices and provide clear opt-out options.

Rigorous testing and quality assurance are crucial. Thoroughly test your app to identify and resolve bugs, crashes, or performance issues. A well-tested app is more likely to meet quality standards. Additionally, maintaining detailed documentation of your app's features, data collection practices, and any third-party integrations can be useful during the app review process.

Once your app is submitted to an app store, it undergoes a meticulous review process to ensure compliance with the guidelines. Review times can vary, and patience is essential during this phase. If your app is rejected, app stores provide feedback to help you address the issues and resubmit your app for review. Responding to feedback promptly and making the necessary adjustments is crucial.

Adherence to app store policies requires constant attention and is not a one-time thing. By building a solid reputation for your app and showcasing your commitment to customer satisfaction and data protection, it paves the way for long-term success. Conversely, non-compliance can lead to app rejection, loss of user trust, and even removal from app stores. In an ever-evolving digital landscape, staying compliant is not just a requirement; it's a strategic imperative for app developers seeking long-term success.

User Agreements and Policies

User agreements and policies are the cornerstones of trust and transparency between developers and users in the world of mobile app development. These legal documents —which users frequently ignore—are essential for outlining the parameters of the interaction, outlining obligations, and protecting the interests of both parties.

These agreements—whether they be the Terms of Service (ToS), Privacy Policy, or End-User License Agreement (EULA)—are necessary legal formalities and vital resources for upholding pleasant and knowledgeable interactions in the digital sphere. This section will discuss the importance of user agreements and policies in the creation of mobile apps, including an overview of their main features, recommended procedures, and function in building ethical conduct and trust.

User agreements and policies are the contractual agreements between app developers and users. They outline the rules of engagement, the terms under which users can access and use the app, and the legal framework governing the relationship. While users often accept these agreements without reading them thoroughly, they hold significant legal and ethical weight.

First and foremost, these agreements set the expectations for users. They clarify how users should behave within the app, what constitutes acceptable use, and what actions are prohibited. This clarity is essential for maintaining order, preventing misuse, and protecting the app's integrity.

Moreover, user agreements and policies safeguard users' rights and privacy. They define how user data is collected, processed, and protected, aligning with data protection regulations like GDPR and CCPA. By establishing a transparent framework for data handling, these documents empower users to make informed decisions about their data.

Key components of user agreements and policies include acceptance and consent, user conduct, data usage and privacy, intellectual property, termination and suspension, and dispute resolution.

Best practices for user agreements and policies include clarity and simplicity, transparency, accessibility, update notifications, and consent mechanisms. Keep the language in these documents clear and straightforward to ensure users can easily understand their rights and obligations. Be transparent about data practices and how user data will be used, and make these documents easily accessible within the app. Notify users of any changes to the agreements or policies, and implement precise mechanisms for users to consent to the agreements.

User agreements and policies are central to building and maintaining trust between developers and users. Trust is the cornerstone of a successful app-user relationship. When users understand the rules and data handling practices, they are more likely to trust the app with their data and engage with it without reservations.

Furthermore, these documents underscore the developer's commitment to ethical conduct. By setting clear expectations and guidelines for user behavior, app developers create a respectful and inclusive environment within their apps. Users appreciate apps that prioritize their safety, privacy, and overall experience.

In conclusion, user agreements and policies are not merely legal obligations but tools for fostering trust, transparency, and ethical conduct in the mobile app development landscape. Developers should approach the creation of these documents with care, ensuring clarity, transparency, and accessibility. By doing so, they fulfill legal requirements and lay the foundation for strong, respectful, and lasting relationships with their users.

CHAPTER XI

Case Studies and Success Stories

Real-World Examples of Successful Apps

A small number of apps have stood out in the ever-evolving world of mobile app development, capturing the attention of users and having a big influence on our daily life. These success stories show how creative thinking, user-centered design, and well-executed strategy can take an app to new heights and are a testament to the endless possibilities in the app market. This section will explore real-world examples of successful apps, shedding light on their key features, the strategies that contributed to their success, and the lessons they offer to aspiring app developers.

One example is WhatsApp, the brainchild of Jan Koum and Brian Acton, which revolutionized communication by offering a secure, user-friendly messaging platform. Its ease of use and dedication to consumer privacy are the reasons behind its success. WhatsApp made sure that messages were private and secure by highlighting end-to-end encryption, a feature that is highly regarded in a time when concerns about digital privacy are on the rise. Its popularity was further aided by its early lack of advertisements and cross-platform compatibility.

The creation of Instagram by Mike Krieger and Kevin Systrom revolutionized the way we share and interact with visual content. Its emphasis on user interaction and visual narrative is what makes it successful. Users found it simple to take, edit, and share pictures and videos on Instagram due to its simple and user-friendly design. Its user base increased through partnerships with businesses and influencers, while features like Stories and Explore kept consumers interested.

Uber upended the taxi business by providing a dependable, affordable, and easy-to-use ride-sharing service. Its ability to solve a common problem—hailing a cab—and deliver a flawless solution through an intuitive app was crucial to its success. Uber's driver rating system, cashless payment options, and real-time tracking guaranteed passenger convenience and safety.

Spotify completely changed the music industry by providing a vast streaming library of songs, playlists, and podcasts. Its freemium business strategy, which allowed users to browse a sizable repertoire with advertisements or subscribe for an ad-free experience, is responsible for its success. Listeners were kept interested with personalized playlists and recommendations depending on their tastes.

Niantic's Pokémon GO brought augmented reality (AR) gaming into the mainstream. By combining the beloved Pokémon franchise with real-world exploration, the app captured the imagination of millions. Its success stemmed from its innovative use of AR technology, encouraging players to explore their surroundings while capturing virtual creatures.

These real-world success stories offer valuable insights for aspiring app developers. They emphasize the importance of solving real-world problems, prioritizing user-centric design, ensuring privacy and security, and exploring creative ways to engage users and monetize the app. Innovation, effective marketing, partnerships, and a commitment to continuous improvement are also key factors in achieving app success.

In conclusion, the success stories of WhatsApp, Instagram, Uber, Spotify, and Pokémon GO serve as beacons of inspiration for app developers. They remind us that success in the app industry is not limited to established giants but can be achieved through innovative ideas, user-centric design, and a commitment to addressing real-world problems. By drawing insights from these examples and embracing key strategies, aspiring app developers can embark on their journeys toward creating impactful and successful apps that leave a lasting mark on users' lives.

What You Can Learn from Their Journeys

The journey from a concept to a successful mobile app is often paved with challenges, creative breakthroughs, and strategic decisions. The stories of successful apps like WhatsApp, Instagram, Uber, Spotify, and Pokémon GO offer invaluable insights into the world of app development. They showcase the possibilities within the app industry and provide a blueprint for aspiring developers and entrepreneurs. In this section, we will delve into what you can learn from their journeys, highlighting key takeaways that can guide you on your path to app development success.

One of the common threads among these successful apps is their unwavering commitment to user-centric design. They prioritize user experience above all else, creating intuitive, visually appealing interfaces, and easy to navigate. Whether it's Instagram's clean and simple photo-sharing interface or Uber's user-friendly ride-hailing process, these apps ensure that users can easily understand and use their platforms. This is a lesson that aspiring developers should remember: the success of your app hinges on how well it meets the specific requirements and tastes of your intended user base.

Successful apps often emerge from a keen understanding of real-world problems and developing solutions that make users' lives easier or more enjoyable. Uber, for example, identified the challenge of hailing taxis and transformed it into a convenient, cost-effective ride-sharing service. Pokémon GO tapped into the desire for outdoor exploration and nostalgia for the beloved Pokémon franchise. These apps resonated with users profoundly by addressing tangible pain points or desires. As an aspiring developer, seek out genuine problems your app can solve or unmet needs.

Innovation is a driving force behind app success. Whether it's WhatsApp's emphasis on secure, encrypted messaging or Spotify's introduction of a freemium model for music streaming, these apps pushed the boundaries of what was possible in their respective niches. They set themselves apart from competitors by embracing new technologies, features, or business models. As an app developer, don't shy away from innovation. Explore emerging trends, technologies, and creative solutions to stand out in the crowded app market.

Building a great app is only part of the equation; effective marketing and partnerships are crucial in reaching a broader audience. Instagram's collaborations with influencers and brands helped it gain traction, while Pokémon GO's strategic partnership with Nintendo leveraged an existing fan base. Marketing efforts should be well-targeted, engaging, and aligned with your app's unique selling points.

Successful apps prioritize data privacy and security in an era of heightened privacy concerns. For instance, WhatsApp's implementation of end-to-end encryption reassured users that their messages were safe from prying eyes. As an app developer, consider how to protect user data and communicate your commitment to privacy and security transparently.

The journey of app development is ongoing. Continuous iteration and improvement are essential for staying relevant and meeting evolving user needs. These successful apps didn't rest on their laurels; they actively listened to user feedback and made enhancements accordingly. Be prepared to adapt and refine your app as you receive insights from your user base.

In conclusion, the journeys of successful apps like WhatsApp, Instagram, Uber, Spotify, and Pokémon GO offer a wealth of insights for aspiring app developers. User-centric design, problem-solving, innovation, effective marketing, data privacy, and ongoing improvement are among the key lessons they impart. While each app's story is unique, the principles they embody can guide your path to app development success. By combining these lessons with your creativity, passion, and dedication, you can embark on your own journey, with the potential to create an app that leaves a lasting impact on users and the digital landscape.

Inspirational Stories

Mobile app development is a dynamic field that continually offers inspiring stories of triumph, innovation, and resilience. Behind each successful app lies a journey characterized by passion, persistence, and the pursuit of a vision. In this section, we will explore some inspirational stories in mobile app development, shedding light on the developers' motivations, the challenges they faced, and the valuable lessons they offer to those seeking to make their mark in the industry.

One such inspiring story is the journey of "Angry Birds," developed by Rovio Entertainment, a small Finnish company. What began as a modest project led by developers Niklas Hed, Jarno Väkeväinen, and Jaakko Iisalo faced numerous rejections before securing funding. However, the team's belief in the game's potential and their unwavering persistence paid off, turning "Angry Birds" into a global franchise encompassing merchandise, movies, and theme parks. This story teaches us the vital lesson that persistence and belief in your idea can lead to extraordinary success.

Another remarkable tale is the rise of "Instagram" from its 2010 launch to becoming one of the world's most popular social media platforms. Co-founders Kevin Systrom and Mike Krieger began with a simple concept: sharing photos with friends. They focused on creating an elegant and user-friendly platform, constantly iterating based on user feedback. After a series of updates and strategic moves, such as launching on Android, Instagram rapidly grew its user base and was eventually acquired by Facebook for a billion dollars. This story underscores the importance of refining your app based on user needs and staying adaptable in a rapidly changing tech landscape.

"Candy Crush Saga," developed by the Swedish gaming company King, is another inspirational journey. King faced numerous rejections before the game's breakthrough. What set "Candy Crush" apart was its combination of addictive gameplay, social features, and the freemium model. This model allowed users to play for free while offering the option to purchase in-game items.

The game's success reinforced the idea that innovative monetization models can coexist with enjoyable user experiences.

Duolingo's founder, Luis von Ahn, envisioned making education accessible to everyone. He created "Duolingo," a language learning app that gamified the process, making it engaging and free of charge. This unique approach to education resonated with users, and Duolingo rapidly grew in popularity. The app's success demonstrates that a noble mission and innovative gamification can change how we learn.

The story of "Snapchat" is a testament to the power of bold ideas. Co-founder Evan Spiegel envisioned a platform where messages disappeared after being viewed—a concept met with skepticism and ridicule. Despite the challenges, Spiegel and his team persisted. Snapchat became a hit among younger users and became a multimedia platform with Stories and Discover. This story teaches us that disruptive ideas can reshape industries, even when they challenge convention.

These inspirational stories from the world of mobile app development share common themes: the importance of believing in your idea, user-centric design, adapting to change, innovative monetization, and the potential for disruptive ideas to change the game. They also highlight the significance of persistence and resilience in facing challenges.

In conclusion, the world of mobile app development is ripe with inspirational stories that demonstrate the limitless potential of human creativity and innovation. Whether you're a budding app developer or simply someone who appreciates the impact of technology on our lives, these stories remind you that with the right idea, passion, and determination, you can create an app that leaves a lasting mark on the world. The key is to stay inspired, stay adaptable, and never stop pursuing your vision.

CHAPTER XII

Future Trends in Mobile App Development

Emerging Technologies (AR/VR, AI, IoT)

As a result of the speed at which emerging technologies are developing, the field of mobile app development is always changing. Artificial Intelligence (or AI), the Internet of Things (or IoT), and Augmented and Virtual Reality (AR/VR) are three major areas that have had a big impact on the industry. This section will examine these innovative technologies, their effects on the creation of mobile apps, and the fascinating opportunities they present to both consumers and developers.

Virtual reality (also known as VR) and augmented reality (also known as AR) are game-changing technologies that have expanded the immersive possibilities of mobile apps. Virtual reality (VR) provides fully immersive virtual settings, whereas augmented reality (AR) overlays digital content onto the actual world to enhance users' perspective of their surroundings. Mobile apps like Pokémon GO exemplify the potential of AR, allowing users to interact with virtual creatures in their surroundings, merging the digital and physical worlds. Conversely, VR powers apps like Oculus, providing users with immersive gaming and entertainment experiences where they are transported to entirely virtual realms. Beyond gaming, these technologies hold immense potential in education, healthcare, training, and more. Mobile app developers increasingly leverage AR and VR to create captivating, interactive, and educational experiences that redefine user engagement.

Artificial Intelligence (AI) is another transformative force in mobile app development. AI has empowered mobile apps to become more intelligent, responsive, and capable of understanding and anticipating user needs. AI-driven chatbots in customer service apps provide instant assistance to users, streamlining support processes. Voice assistants like Siri and Google Assistant rely on AI for natural language processing, offering voice-controlled interactions and making tasks more convenient for users. Furthermore, AI's ability to analyze vast amounts of user data and behavior enables apps to deliver personalized content and recommendations, enhancing the overall user experience. As AI technologies advance, mobile app developers gain access to increasingly sophisticated tools and libraries, enabling them to create apps that offer enhanced functionality, automation, and personalization.

The Internet of Things (IoT) is yet another frontier that profoundly impacts mobile app development. IoT represents the connection of physical objects to the digital world, and mobile apps serve as crucial interfaces for controlling and monitoring IoT devices. For example, smart home apps allow users to remotely control lights, thermostats, and security systems using their smartphones. Healthcare apps can collect and transmit vital data from wearable IoT devices to healthcare providers, facilitating remote monitoring and personalized care. The potential applications of IoT in mobile app development extend across various industries, including agriculture, transportation, and manufacturing. Mobile app developers are essential to the growth of the Internet of Things ecosystem because they design smart and user-friendly apps that maximize the capabilities of connected devices.

These new technologies have enormous ramifications for the creation of mobile apps, giving developers the chance to make creative, captivating, and extremely functional apps that meet a variety of user requirements. By utilizing these technologies, developers can create engaging user experiences, improve user engagement by means of automation and personalization, and take advantage of the enormous potential of the Internet of Things ecosystem. Since the world of mobile app development is still developing rapidly, it is imperative that you keep up with the most recent developments in these technologies. As developers harness the potential of AR/VR, AI, and IoT, we can anticipate a future where mobile apps become even more powerful, immersive, and indispensable in our daily lives, opening up new horizons of possibilities for users and developers alike.

Evolving User Behavior and Expectations

The past decade have seen a significant transformation in the mobile app market due to both shifting user behavior and quick technological improvements. With the increasing integration of smartphones into our everyday routines, our expectations for mobile apps have changed. This section will examine how the mobile app market is shaped by changing user expectations and behavior, as well as how developers must adjust to satisfy these shifting needs.

One of the most significant shifts in user behavior is the growing reliance on mobile apps for various tasks and activities. Mobile apps have gone beyond mere convenience; they have become essential tools for communication, entertainment, productivity, and even healthcare. Users now expect apps to seamlessly integrate into their daily routines, simplifying tasks and providing value. Whether it's messaging apps for instant communication, fitness apps for tracking health, or banking apps for managing finances, users increasingly rely on apps to enhance their lives.

Users' expectations for app performance and usability have risen significantly as they become more discerning. Slow-loading apps, frequent crashes, and unintuitive interfaces are no longer tolerated. Users demand apps that are fast, stable, and user-friendly. Any friction or frustration in the user experience can result in immediate uninstallation and a negative review. Consequently, developers must prioritize performance optimization, rigorous testing, and user-centered design to ensure their apps meet these heightened expectations.

Another notable change in user behavior is the desire for personalized experiences. Users expect apps to tailor content, recommendations, and interactions to their preferences and behaviors. This personalization extends across various app categories, from social media platforms curating news feeds to e-commerce apps offering personalized product recommendations. Machine learning and AI-driven algorithms are crucial in delivering these personalized experiences by analyzing user data and adapting app content accordingly.

Security and privacy concerns have also become paramount in users' minds. High-profile data breaches and privacy scandals have made users increasingly cautious about sharing their personal information with apps. Consequently, users expect transparent data collection practices, robust security measures, and the option to control their privacy settings. Developers must prioritize data security, implement stringent privacy policies, and communicate their commitment to safeguarding user data to earn and maintain user trust.

The rise of mobile app stores and app marketplaces has created a crowded and competitive landscape. Users are given various choices within each app category, making first impressions critical. As a result, app store optimization (ASO) has become a vital aspect of app marketing. Developers must invest in ASO strategies to enhance app visibility, improve ratings and reviews, and ensure that their apps stand out amid the competition. User feedback and engagement have also become central to app development. Users expect responsive customer support channels, quick bug fixes, and regular updates that address their concerns and suggestions. In-app feedback mechanisms, customer support chatbots, and social media presence are essential for maintaining a strong connection with users and fostering loyalty.

Lastly, users have grown increasingly conscious of the environmental impact of technology. Sustainable and eco-friendly practices are gaining prominence in the mobile app industry. Users appreciate apps that minimize energy consumption, reduce carbon footprints, and prioritize eco-friendly features.

In conclusion, evolving user behavior and expectations shape the mobile app landscape. Users rely on apps for an ever-widening array of tasks, demand exceptional performance and usability, seek personalized experiences, prioritize security and privacy, consider app store visibility, value responsive support, and appreciate eco-friendly practices. Developers who recognize and adapt to these evolving expectations are better positioned to create apps that resonate with users, stand out in the marketplace, and thrive in an increasingly competitive environment. As technology advances, user behavior and expectations will undoubtedly evolve further, challenging developers to remain agile and innovative in their pursuit of creating exceptional mobile experiences.

Preparing for the Future

The field of mobile app development is always changing due to the quick advancement of technology, changing consumer habits, and dynamic market conditions. In order to thrive in this ever-changing environment, developers need to be ready for the opportunities and difficulties that lie ahead in addition to anticipating and meeting existing expectations. The key techniques and factors to take into account in order to get ready for the future of mobile app development will be discussed in this section.

Using new technology is one of the most important parts of future-proofing your mobile application. The way we engage with mobile apps is changing as a result of technologies like augmented and virtual reality (AR/VR), artificial intelligence, and the Internet of Things. By staying informed about these technologies and exploring their integration into app development, developers can position themselves at the forefront of innovation. AR and VR can create immersive experiences, AI can power intelligent chatbots and personalization, and IoT opens up opportunities to connect and control a wide range of smart devices.

User-centric design remains paramount in the future of app development. User expectations will continue to evolve, demanding apps that are functional, intuitive, personalized, and aesthetically pleasing. Gathering user feedback, conducting usability testing, and continuously refining the user experience are essential practices. Anticipating users' needs and preferences and prioritizing accessibility and inclusivity will be critical in preparing for the future.

As the mobile device landscape diversifies, cross-platform compatibility will become increasingly important. Users may switch between smartphones, tablets, wearables, and even smart TVs seamlessly. Developers should consider building apps that offer consistent experiences across different platforms and screen sizes. Tools like cross-platform development frameworks can streamline this process, ensuring broader reach and adaptability.

Security and privacy will continue to be significant concerns for users. With the growing concern over data breaches and privacy violations, app developers must prioritize security and data protection. Proactively implementing robust security measures, adopting encryption standards, and respecting user privacy preferences will be crucial to maintaining trust.

In a future where app ecosystems are interconnected, collaboration and partnerships can open new avenues for growth. Partnering with complementary apps, services, or platforms can extend the reach and functionality of your app. Collaboration can also be a source of innovation, enabling developers to combine expertise and resources.

In the quick-paced world of mobile app development, lifelong learning is crucial. Staying updated on the latest programming languages, development tools, and best practices is necessary. Additionally, developers should remain adaptable and ready to pivot as market trends shift. Continuous improvement should be a guiding principle in app development.

Lastly, as technology evolves, so do regulations. Developers must remain vigilant to changes in data privacy laws, security standards, and industry-specific regulations. Being prepared to adapt your app and practices to meet new legal requirements is essential to avoid potential setbacks.

In conclusion, preparing for the future in mobile app development is a dynamic and multifaceted endeavor. Embracing emerging technologies, prioritizing user-centric design, ensuring cross-platform compatibility, safeguarding security and privacy, committing to continuous learning, and considering sustainability and ethics are essential strategies. Collaboration and adaptability to regulatory changes will also play pivotal roles in future success. App developers can confidently traverse the constantly changing terrain and create apps that resonate with consumers and last over time in a market that is becoming more competitive and dynamic by implementing these strategies and staying agile.

CONCLUSION

Summarizing the App Development Journey

The app development journey is a remarkable and multifaceted adventure that begins with inspiration and culminates in a tangible product that can impact millions of lives. This section will summarize the stages and key takeaways from the app development journey, highlighting the essential aspects that developers must navigate to bring their ideas to life and create successful mobile applications.

The journey commences with ideation, where developers brainstorm app concepts. This stage is marked by creativity, problem-solving, and exploring unique ideas. Key takeaways include the importance of thorough idea validation, market research, and identifying a target audience to ensure your app addresses a genuine need. Once the app concept is solidified, developers move to the planning and strategy phase. This is where clear objectives, features, and functionality are defined. Crafting a detailed project timeline and budget is crucial for successful execution. Setting measurable goals and aligning the app's purpose with user needs are key takeaways in this stage.

The design and user experience phase focuses on creating an intuitive and visually appealing interface. Incorporating user-centered design principles, wireframing, and prototyping are essential elements. This stage underscores the significance of creating a seamless and enjoyable user journey.

Developers then transition to the development and coding phase, bringing the app's functionalities to life. Selecting the right development team, choosing the appropriate programming language, and deciding between native and cross-platform development are critical considerations. This stage emphasizes the importance of a solid technical foundation.

Thorough testing and quality control are necessary to guarantee that the software is bug-free and operates smoothly. Functional, usability, and performance testing are integral components of this stage. Developers should also prioritize beta testing and user feedback to refine the app further.

The deployment and launch phase involves preparing the app for app stores and submitting it for review. Developers must optimize the app store listing through App Store Optimization (ASO) to maximize visibility. Launch strategies and marketing efforts are crucial to create a strong initial user base.

After the app is live, developers must continue to monitor user feedback and analytics. Continuous improvement and updates are vital to address user needs, fix bugs, and enhance the app's stability. Handling user support and feedback efficiently is an ongoing responsibility.

Scaling the app to accommodate a growing user base and expanding its features and functionalities are key considerations for long-term success. Preparing for scaling challenges, such as server infrastructure and performance optimization, is essential.

Throughout the journey, developers must navigate legal and ethical considerations, including intellectual property rights, privacy, data security, and compliance with app store guidelines. Upholding high ethical standards and ensuring compliance with relevant regulations is a continuous commitment.

The app development journey continues after the launch. Developers must be prepared for the future by embracing emerging technologies, staying adaptable, and preparing for evolving user behaviors and expectations. Lifelong learning and the ability to pivot are vital for future readiness.

In summary, the app development journey is a dynamic and multifaceted process that encompasses ideation, planning, design, development, testing, deployment, post-launch optimization, scaling, legal and ethical considerations, and future readiness. Each stage offers unique challenges and opportunities, and successful app development requires a holistic approach that combines creativity, technical expertise, user-centered design, and a commitment to continuous improvement. While the journey may be complex, it is also immensely rewarding, as developers have the power to create innovative solutions and positively impact the lives of users around the world.

Encouragement and Next Steps

Starting a mobile app development journey is an exciting yet challenging endeavor. You have successfully traversed the challenges of ideation, planning, design, development, testing, deployment, and more throughout your journey. It's critical that you recognize your accomplishments as you stand here and focus on the next moves that will propel your career in this ever-evolving industry.

First and foremost, you should celebrate your accomplishments. Transforming an idea into a fully functional app is a significant achievement. Each stage of development, from concept to launch and post-launch optimization, has been a testament to your dedication and expertise. Take a moment to appreciate your effort and hard work in bringing your vision to life.

However, the app development world is ever-evolving, and new challenges and opportunities are always on the horizon. Here are some encouraging thoughts and next steps to consider:

To keep up with the newest trends and best practices as you traverse the rapidly evolving tech business, think about furthering your knowledge through workshops, online resources, or classes. This dedication to learning will maintain the competitiveness of your apps and your abilities.

Building a professional network in the app development community can be invaluable. Attend conferences, join online forums, and engage with fellow developers. Collaborating with others can lead to fresh ideas, innovative solutions, and potential partnerships that enhance your projects.

Consider diversifying your portfolio by exploring different types of apps or targeting new industries. Experimenting with various app concepts can broaden your skillset and open up new growth opportunities.

Continue to prioritize user feedback and user-centric design. Your apps' success hinges on meeting your audience's needs and expectations. Engaging with users, collecting feedback, and making data-driven improvements will ensure your apps remain relevant and valuable.

Investigate the latest innovations by learning about the Internet of Things (or IoT), augmented reality, virtual reality, and artificial intelligence. These technologies may present intriguing opportunities for your upcoming endeavors.

Because technology is becoming more and more integrated into society, think about the ethical and sustainable aspects of your work. To keep users' trust, adopt eco-friendly procedures, deal with biases in AI systems, and protect user data.

Establish fresh objectives for your app development journey by thinking back on your previous experiences. Having specific goals will help you stay inspired and focused, whether they have to do with finishing a challenging project, reaching a specific user milestone, or contributing to a worthy cause.

Setbacks are a normal part of the development process, and not every program will become a huge success. Recognize failure as a chance to improve and gain knowledge. Whatever the experience—good or bad—it all helps you become a better developer.

Look for a mentor in the field who can offer advice and perspectives from their expertise. A mentor may guide you through challenges, provide insightful counsel, and hasten your career advancement.

In conclusion, your journey in mobile app development is a dynamic and ever-evolving adventure. While celebrating your achievements is essential, looking forward to the next steps is equally crucial. By committing to lifelong learning, expanding your network, embracing emerging technologies, and maintaining a user-centric and ethical approach, you'll be well-prepared to tackle the challenges and opportunities that lie ahead. The world of app development holds limitless possibilities, and with dedication and a forward-thinking mindset, you can continue to make a meaningful impact through your innovative creations.

Final Thoughts

Let's take a minute to appreciate the amazing adventure you have started as we come to the end of our exploration of the mobile app development process. From the first idea to the launch of your app and beyond, this journey has been full of opportunities for growth, challenges to overcome, and inspirational moments. We'll go through the most important lessons learned in these concluding remarks and provide some parting advice to help you in your continued exploration of the app development industry.

Your adventure was sparked by the imaginative potential of ideas. Recall that every great software started out as a mere thought, and that ideas are the seeds of creativity. Continue to foster your imagination, and don't be scared to investigate even the most bizarre ideas—innovation frequently comes from the unexpected.

The development process undoubtedly presented its share of challenges, from coding hurdles to design dilemmas and testing tribulations. Yet, your ability to persevere and find solutions is a testament to your resilience. Know that challenges are opportunities in disguise, and each obstacle you overcame has strengthened your skills.

The tech world is in constant motion, with new technologies, devices, and trends emerging regularly. Embrace change and stay adaptable. By keeping your finger on the pulse of industry shifts, you'll position yourself to seize new opportunities and remain a leader in the field.

Throughout your journey, user-centricity has been a guiding principle. Continue to put your users at the forefront of your development process. Their feedback and needs should steer the direction of your work. Listen, learn, and iterate to create experiences that genuinely resonate with your audience.

Learning more about app development is a never-ending quest. Regardless of your level of experience, make a commitment to lifelong learning as a developer. Learn new programming languages, explore the latest innovations, and keep improving your skills. You can add more to your projects as you gain more knowledge.

App development doesn't happen in isolation. It thrives in a community of like-minded individuals. Collaborate, share your experiences, and learn from others. Remember that building connections can lead to unexpected opportunities and fresh insights.

As an app developer, you have the power to create solutions that can impact lives. With that power comes responsibility. Prioritize ethical practices, consider sustainability, and protect user data. Upholding high ethical standards is essential in building trust.

Finally, cherish the joys of innovation. The thrill of seeing your app come to life, the excitement of user engagement, and the satisfaction of overcoming challenges make this journey genuinely remarkable. Keep that passion alive as you continue to innovate and shape the future of app development.

In conclusion, developing mobile apps is an exciting, rewarding, and always changing experience. You've come this far due to your perseverance, creativity, and dedication, and there are countless opportunities ahead of you. It doesn't matter if you are an experienced developer or are just getting started—every step you take will help you contribute to the constantly changing field of technology and have a positive influence. Savor the delight of creating, enjoy every second of this journey, and never stop pushing the limits of what's feasible in the world of mobile apps. You are just getting started on an amazing and life-changing career path in app development, so your journey is far from over.

Thank you for buying and reading/ listening to our book. If you found this book useful/ helpful please take a few minutes and leave a review on the platform where you purchased our book. Your feedback matters greatly to us.

www.ingramcontent.com/pod-product-compliance
Lightning Source LLC
Chambersburg PA
CBHW071512150726
48000CB00002B/559